By Hook
or
By Crook

How Cults Lure Christians

By Hook
or
By Crook

How Cults Lure Christians

Harold L. Busséll

McCracken Press
New York

McCracken Press™
An imprint of Multi Media Communicators, Inc.
575 Madison Avenue, Suite 1006
New York, NY 10022

Cover Illustration, Tim Ladwig.

Library of Congress Catalog Card Number: 93-078995

ISBN 1-56977-585-0

10 9 8 7 6 5 4 3 2 1

Printed in the United States of America

To my wife Carol and
my children Monique and Bradford,
without whose encouragement
I would never have
finished this book.

Contents

Preface

This book is not an attack on either cults or Christians. It is an examination of the things cultists and Christians hold in common. Many Christians assail the false teachings of the cults, but there are several dangers inherent in a one-sided approach to heretical teachings. First, we Christians may become blinded to the qualities we revere as signs of spirituality, and this, if not understood, can make us susceptible to cults and aberrant religious groups.

Second, in our fight against deception and false teaching, we can easily attack people instead of problems and thus lose opportunities for ministry. We can also use our insights to excuse sinful pride, insensitivity, and lack of compassion.

God's Word calls us to think critically of the world in which we live and to discern the false teachings that seek to pull us off center. There is a danger, however, of becoming critical, attacking people, blind to our own weaknesses and vulnerabilities. We must be careful lest we step over the fine line that changes us from critical thinkers into critical people.

I am concerned that we view the insights in this book through eyeglasses tinted with compassionate service to confused and hurting people who desperately need genuine concern and love.

The issues presented in these pages have been born in my own struggles and questions and from my relationships with many who have completed a painful, long, emotional, and fearful journey back to stability after being involved in an aberrant religious group. All these people were raised in Christian homes and have returned to faith in Jesus Christ.

It is important to note that there are several definitions of the word *cult* popular today. The word *cult* simply means "worship." There are, however, basically three definitions of the word currently in use in our culture. First is the sociological definition that tends to define a cult primarily in terms of style and psychosocial dynamics of control and abuse. Second is the popular definition coming through the media that tends to focus on the sensational and the bizarre. Third, traditionally, the term *cult* has been used to define groups that veer away from the belief system of one of the major religions. In other words, there exist Islamic cults, Hindu cults, as well as Christian cults.

Many groups on the religious landscape that have traditionally been defined as cults doctrinally do not abuse their members in aberrant ways. An increasing number of groups that are thoroughly Christian in belief, however, are using aberrational methods of control and in that sense fall into the category of a cult from a psychosocial perspective.

For simplicity's sake in this book, I will use the word *cult* in a religious sense to refer to those groups that call themselves Christian and hold beliefs and practices clearly in opposition to historic Christianity as expressed in the Apostles' Creed.

My deepest thanks are due to those who encouraged and pushed me to write this book—my wife Carol, Gigi Tchividjian, and Ruth Dienert.

By Hook
or
By Crook

1

Thank God I Am Not One of Them —or Could I Be?

What happened to John Moriconi? If it happened to him, could it happen to you?

John was an Evangelical Christian, a good Baptist. But then he spent eight years as a leader in the Children of God. Eight long years, before he left.

When I met him, he was a student at Gordon College, where I served as Dean of the Chapel. Our long discussions of his past involvement with the Children of God and of his present search for God always left me thoroughly puzzled, yet fascinated. He had never wavered in his primary purpose: He sincerely desired to know God's truth and to relate personally to

Jesus Christ. Yet his search had led him down a path that ended in the cultic community.

"How?" I wondered. "Why?"

John finally saw that the Children of God did not offer him the truth for which he longed. He has written a booklet entitled *Children of God, Family of Love*[1] to help others who have followed the same path as he, for he realized (and he has shown me) that he is not alone in his misguided search.

We who sit on padded church pews may think that those "deluded, crazy cult members" are people who were previously unchurched pagans.

Many of them are, but let's look a little closer.

I counseled one young woman over a period of time. I uncovered that she had difficulties making decisions, troubles with severe depression, doubts concerning her faith, and an inability to cope with life. She related to me her background: raised in a prominent Evangelical church, knew the Scriptures, led Bible studies, had introduced many friends to Jesus Christ. But then her problems began. Her family became involved in an Evangelical community with cultic leanings. They were not alone in their decision, as many members of their church, including the pastor, joined the questionable group. They sold their homes. They dropped close friends. Eventually children were separated from their parents and reared by "more spiritual" parents. In group sessions, individuals were pressured publicly to confess attitudes, sexual fantasies, and past sins.

For this young woman, these years were full of confusion, pain, and hurts that caused her journey back to stability to be long and treacherous.

Three other Christians, the mother and two sisters of Akiko Lrick, joined a Korean cult. At a church conference in upstate New York, Akiko told me about her family in Japan. Her mother and sisters had been active for years in a Japanese Evangelical church. Later she wrote me a letter.

"My sisters in their music college days were active in Campus Crusade. They were both promising students in the two most reputable music schools in Japan. Then all of a sudden they found a 'better way' to dedicate more totally to the 'promise' of eradicating the sinful nature. They clearly believe they can achieve sinless states here and now following the Moon recipe for salvation—gaining three men and three women converts to start with, for that is a major ingredient among others—and that their offspring are born without sinful natures for the parents are Moonies and married by the dictate of Mr. Moon. They were married to their men not knowing even the names of their future husbands in mass weddings of three thousands couples at once!! in Seoul, Korea, some seven years ago. They have been in this movement for a good twelve years now.

"Five years ago they had a huge expensive one-week retreat for the family—nonbelievers—in Honolulu, to which I was enticed. But, when unconverted even after all that, I was found 'dead' by my sisters and to a lamentable degree by my mother."

These three women were searching for fellowship and an answer to the problem of sin. Where did they end up? As active leaders in the Unification Church.

Several years later, I met an acquaintance whom I hadn't seen for more than ten years. He told me that his wife, raised in an Assemblies of God missionary's home, had been an active member of the People's Temple led by the Reverend Jim Jones. I am sure many pastors could draw from their journals similar accounts and stories. They have no doubt faced the same questions and confusions as I: Why are we prey to cults and aberrant groups?

Most available books, workshops, and seminars on cults are built around a we/they mentality that contrasts their heretical doctrines against the biblical truths on which we stand. Until recently even my own focus has been on the error and corruption of their teachings.

But are other issues involved?

In all my discussions with people allured by cults, I have talked to only one person whose attraction centered on doctrine. Because doctrine was so seldom mentioned, I was forced to reexamine my past discussions and ask whether or not Christians are particularly susceptible to cults.

After much thought, reflection, and discussion, I faced the evidence: Yes, we are vulnerable.

I looked back on my twenty-seven years of ministry in California, Europe, and New England, and I reconstructed my conversations with those who had come out of a cult, had family members in cults, or were attending cultic or aberrant groups out of curiosity. Definite and similar patterns of thought kept recurring, as steadily as a ticking metronome. Christians do have something in common with cults: zeal and confidence. We cherish and value similar signs of spirituality. Many of us share with them similar ideas concerning authority, loyalty, and submission.

A close examination of popular Western cults reveals that many began in an Evangelical Christian church or under leaders who claimed Christianity—men and women from solid church backgrounds.

Sun Myung Moon, founder of the Unification Church, was reared in a Presbyterian home. Jim Jones, founder of the People's Temple, at one time attended a Nazarene church; later he pastored an interdenominational church and a Disciples of Christ congregation. Moses David (David Berg), founder of the Children of God, is the son of Evangelical parents, served as a minister in a Christian and Missionary Alliance church, and was involved for a time in a Christian television ministry. Victor Paul Wierwille, founder of The Way, came out of the Reformed Church, where he served as pastor to a number of active congregations; during the forties he served as an adjunct professor of New Testament at a leading Evangelical Christian college.

Many of the white woodframe churches that dot the New England countryside are

Unitarian. At one time in their history almost all these churches were Trinitarian, biblical, and parishes of Congregational, Baptist, or Episcopal denominations. Mary Baker Eddy, founder of the Christian Scientists, and Charles Taze Russell, founder of the Jehovah's Witnesses, were both raised in markedly Christian homes and churches.

While it is easy and comfortable for us to think in terms of "them" and "us"—being thankful that we are not one of them—the fact is that many of them used to be one with us. Might we Christians be more myopic than we realize? Might we need to expand our field of vision and note that our sense of security and offensive attacks on their doctrines are blinding us? It is time we read carefully the fine print of past decades.

In our fervor to point out errors of doctrine, we have virtually ignored our own shortcomings and vulnerabilities. Remember, former Evangelical Christians died in Jonestown and currently are active in the Unification Church, The Way, the Children of God, and other heretical or aberrant groups.

It is easy for us, as churches and as individuals, to put on our doctrinal sunglasses and squint our eyes so as to block these issues from our sight. But in doing so, we only remove the reminder of our responsibility to face our own susceptibility to cultic deception.

Perhaps we should pray that God will give us full sight and remove our arrogant attitudes. Too many of our soldiers have fallen for us to feel that our battle lines are impenetrable. The fallen could be one of us.

2

But You Can See the Love on Their Faces

"**I**'ve found new life. Joy. Happiness. Purpose. Love."

"I've given up my drug habit. My immorality. My old sinful habits."

Such testimonies are frequently touted by Christians: "Because we have experienced, we know." But we are far from alone in our assurances. Cult members also boast of changed lives and spiritual trophies.

Our emphasis on subjective religious experience has caused many secular observers to confuse Evangelical Christians with other "radical" religious groups who also exhibit changed lives, testimonies of joy, smiling faces, and evangelistic zeal.

Our overemphasis on subjective experience has some of its roots in our strong reaction against the rationalism, naturalism, and liberalism that infiltrated many Protestant denominations over the past decades. In reaction many people who lacked an in-depth personal apologetic, verification of their faith became a matter of subjective and experiential witness. They felt good all over when someone announced, "I'm not prepared to argue doctrine. All I know is I am a new person." Such a safe retreat could not be challenged intellectually.

But is this sort of defense really safe? Many of the gospel songs written during the last five or six decades reflect the importance placed on this subjective approach to faith and life. A perfect and familiar example is a line from "He Lives" by Alfred H. Ackley: "You ask me how I know He lives? He lives within my heart." But we are facing cults and aberrant groups who use these same terms. They boast of their results, speak of changed lives, even sing these same gospel songs.

Several years ago I curiously watched a Sunday morning gospel television program filmed in Florida. The music was moving and well-presented. The stories were challenging. One young person's inspiring testimony encouraged others to accept Christ, the giver of happiness, joy, and peace. Wanting to see what the other channels presented, I turned the dial. To my surprise, I saw and heard a former antiwar activist sharing almost the same testimony. He claimed he had found the truth, accompanied by unbelievable peace and joy. He saw that his sixties' search really had been a hunger and thirst for a deeper spiritual life. He was now clean-shaven, wearing a stylish suit, and beamed a smile similar to the student on the other program. He even promised the viewer the same fulfilled life.

Spiritually I was deeply moved while listening to his tale of transformation from a life of drugs and angry activism. But as he drew his remarks to a close, he encouraged the audience to contact a local meditation group and there find the same peace, joy, and spiritual blessings he had discovered. I hated to admit it, but until the "sponsor" of the program was identified, I could tell no difference between the attitudes, promised results, or quality and genuineness of conversion of the two speakers.

I know many people who have attended est [Erhard Sensitivity Training], New Age seminars, encounter groups, and people who have converted to cults. They have experienced moral and positive character changes similar to yours or mine. But does "similar" mean "the same as"?

Of course not. Let's look at what really happens to these people.

The Big Difference—The Gospel

As Christians we often bear witness to the results of the gospel rather than to the gospel itself. To do so exclusively is a serious mistake, for it is amazingly easy to confuse various ideological conversion experiences with the true new birth.

Many people undergo dramatic experiences as they are converted to a religious group, an encounter group, a meditation group, or an aberrant religious community. All conversion experiences offer common psychological results. The discovery of a "new life" or a new system for belief gives a fresh reason for living and an exciting focus for life. A new sense of emotional security is born, and its breath is full of direction, a sense of belonging, and often happiness.

But the new birth that is believed and known in the historic faith is a result of the work of the Spirit of God who enables us to acknowledge our sins and confess Jesus Christ as Lord.

The new birth is not based on feelings, but on our coming into union with the resurrected Christ—not just any Christ, but Jesus Christ who is divine and human at once.

Feelings that accompany conversion to Jesus Christ may be positive or negative. To the rich, young ruler who turned away from Christ (Luke 18:18-27), the results of conversion appeared negative and costly. Jesus asked that he leave his materialistic god, his personal possessions.

Frequently we stretch the biblical data to state that the results of true conversion to Christ will all be positive, that our conversion will be accompanied by astounding personal success. As a high school student in 1957, I attended a youth rally in Sacramento, California, in which the guest speaker was a recently converted national beauty queen. In her testimony she attributed all of her success to her faith in Jesus Christ. I then wondered if her conversion was the only reason for her success. During her talk I repeatedly remembered her vital statistics, which had been printed in the previous week's Sacramento Bee. Had they not been a factor?

What about the other Christians in the contest? Did they lack faith, or bust lines?

I had brought a nonbelieving friend to the meeting in hopes of introducing her to Christ. She struggled with self-esteem, was about ninety pounds overweight, and convinced herself she was dying of terminal acne. During the testimony she quietly whispered to me, "If I accept Christ, do you think God would help me become a beauty queen?"

Our testimonies can not only confuse seekers, but can also lay tremendous guilt on people who can't live up to the ideal Christian model set before them. Conversion stories are often punctuated with successes and promises that all problems will be resolved as easily and quickly as on a thirty-minute television show.

How do we sort out the differences between a witness such as the former activist and the young person on the gospel program? How do we separate the promises of success from the realities of living in a fallen world? Were the witnesses of the young woman on the television program and the converted beauty queen really the gospel? If results in our lives or our hearts are the gospel, then the political activist's experience with meditation is also the gospel, because the criterion is change instead of Christ. This is a most confusing matter for us Christians. Continually I meet

believers who condemn themselves because
their experience of Christ doesn't seem quite
as vibrant or successful as someone else's.

Do you ever wonder if you are useless to
God because you have no great spiritual experience about which you can boast? Do you
ever feel like a second-class Christian because
you have some difficult habit, sin, or problem
you can't overcome? If so, you may be susceptible to a cult that will promise you
"results." Cults and other aberrant groups
always offer that something more that seems to
be lacking.

Perhaps contemporary Christian biographies
are so popular because they are exciting and
carry with them secrets on how to fulfill our
unrealistic expectations of what conversion
should be. Many books of this kind give
glowing reports of clean slates and new hearts
before or instead of a holistic and scriptural
picture of Jesus Christ and the Christian Walk.

Biblical believers struggled with their lives,
imperfections, and even failures. David, a
great leader used by God, had moral problems
and difficulties as a father at various times.
Moses was called by God, but still fought with
his flaring temper. Paul and Peter had a disagreement over Peter's following the Galatians

away from the gospel. Paul, Mark, and
Barnabas parted ways because of differences.
God's Word presents a larger picture than we
often allow ourselves to see. Hebrews 11, the
great Faith Chapter, does not talk of faith in
the context of "success." It says that many "by
faith" were beaten, stoned, sawn in half,
tempted, afflicted, and socially rejected.

Testimonies Are Not the Gospel

The testimonies of the young woman on the
television program and the beauty queen were
not the gospel.

Matthew 3:2 says: "Repent, for the kingdom
of heaven is near." Jesus Christ entered human
history in the Incarnation, lived, died, and rose
from the dead so that we might enter that kingdom. The Lord Jesus promised, "Whoever
believes and is baptized will be saved" (Mark
16:16). When we, through trust, are thus
brought into union with Christ our Savior, we
can stand totally forgiven and justified before a
righteous and holy God. We take our place in
His church, where we can be nourished and
built up in the faith. The results felt or seen
after true new birth vary considerably among
individuals, and they must not be presented as
the gospel. God's work by the Holy Spirit in

me differs from the work of the Holy Spirit in another Christian. There are a variety of gifts and effects. For in Christ, we will be led into the change of heart that results from conversion—in fact, conversion means change. But we must remember that these changes are not the gospel. The gospel is something objective and outside of us—complete and finished in Jesus Christ. The gospel is not established by our feelings, moods, or changes, however valid they may be.

When we confuse the results with the message, we tend to remove the basis of Christian living from faith in Christ. Guilt then creeps in and pushes us to compare ourselves with the most current religious hero. Karl Marx once said, "The Christian world is only a reflection of the real world." Perhaps he understood us better than we do.

Often we dress up the latest fad and attach Bible verses to it. In the fifties the secular cry was for light-hearted fun, Ivy League clothes, and happy times. Ours was the "abundant life in Jesus." The sixties called for social revolution: Evangelical books and posters soon boasted of titles like *Jesus the Revolutionary.* The culture of the seventies and eighties turned to T-groups and psychological encounter cells;

of course, we "discovered" relational theology.
In the nineties the call is to self-esteem. The
secular culture of the nineties emphasizes
twelve-step programs; Christian culture has
spawned Christian twelve-step programs. It is
devastating, however, when we insist on living
at the reflective edge of culture in the area of
experience.

Consider this: Beauty queens and athletes
were the attractive Christian flag-bearers of the
fifties. In the sixties the spotlight turned to
converted activists; in the seventies, to transformed drug addicts; and now again, to sports
figures, politicians, and entertainers. If we
continue on this path of trendy Christianity
and pop religion, we will keep on evoking
tremendous insecurity among "normal"
Christians who feel their experience of Jesus
Christ is inadequate. These people are then
tempted to run to a cult for help.

In contrast to modern testimonies, let us
look at conversion and faith in several biblical
accounts. I think first of the dialogue between
Christ and the disciples when He entrusted
them with power to perform great miracles.

> The seventy-two returned with joy
> and said, "Lord, even the demons
> submit to us in your name."

He replied, "I saw Satan fall like lightning from heaven. I have given you authority to trample on snakes and scorpions and to overcome all the power of the enemy; nothing will harm you. However, do not rejoice that the spirits submit to you, but rejoice that your names are written in heaven" (Luke 10: 17-20).

The lesson is so very clear. The Lord Jesus encouraged His disciples to rejoice, not in the spectacular results of an authoritative ministry, but rather in the good news that they had been accepted by the mercy of God. In Scripture, conversion experiences and responses to the gospel vary. Paul experienced a dramatic conversion.

As he neared Damascus on his journey, suddenly a light from heaven flashed around him. He fell to the ground and heard a voice say to him, "Saul, Saul, why do you persecute me?"

"Who are you, Lord?" Saul asked.

"I am Jesus, whom you are persecuting," he replied.

> Then Ananias went to the house
> and entered it. Placing his hands on
> Saul, he said, "Brother Saul, the
> Lord—Jesus, who appeared to you
> on the road as you were coming
> here—has sent me so that you may
> see again and be filled with the Holy
> Spirit." Immediately, something like
> scales fell from Saul's eyes, and he
> could see again (Acts 9:3-5, 17-18).

For Paul the change was dramatic. But by
contrast, Timothy grew gradually into the faith
through family instruction.

> I have been reminded of your sin-
> cere faith, which first lived in your
> grandmother Lois and in your mother
> Eunice and, I am persuaded, now
> lives in you also (2 Timothy 1:5).

Early Leaders Never Confused
Conversion and Rebirth

On Pentecost, Peter made sure that accounts
of conversion and saving faith were connected
directly to the message of the gospel, although
he affirmed the experiential response of the
people as a gift from God. After Pentecost he

did not encourage people to follow Christ for
the experiential benefits of the faith. Instead
Peter preached the historical, crucified, and
resurrected Christ.

"In the last days, God says,
I will pour out my Spirit on all people.
Your sons and daughters will prophesy,
your young men will see visions,
your old men will dream dreams.
Even on my servants, both men and
    women,
I will pour out my Spirit in those days,
and they will prophesy.
I will show wonders in the heaven
above and signs on the earth below,
blood and fire and billows of smoke.
The sun will be turned to darkness
and the moon to blood
before the coming of the great and
glorious day of the Lord.
And everyone who calls
on the name of the Lord will be saved.

"Men of Israel, listen to this: Jesus of
Nazareth was a man accredited by God
to you by miracles, wonders and signs,
which God did among you through him,
as you yourselves know. This man was

handed over to you by God's set purpose and foreknowledge; and you, with the help of wicked men, put him to death by nailing him to the cross. But God raised him from the dead, freeing him from the agony of death, because it was impossible for death to keep its hold on him. . . .

"Therefore, let all Israel be assured of this. God has made this Jesus, whom you crucified, both Lord and Christ" (Acts 2: 17-24, 36)."

When Peter clearly preached Christ, the crowd responded by asking, "What shall we do?" (v. 37). Peter responded:

"Repent and be baptized, every one of you, in the name of Jesus Christ so that your sins may be forgiven. And you will receive the gift of the Holy Spirit. The promise is for you and your children and for all who are far off—for all whom the Lord our God will call" (Acts 2:38-39).

Peter was not satisfied to give witness only to the experience itself. He affirmed the miraculous, but preached the gospel of Jesus

Christ as his basis for calling his listeners to repentance.

The same pattern ensued in Acts 3. When Peter and John healed a beggar at the temple gate, the onlooking crowd grew curious and excited. They wanted to set Peter and John on spiritual pedestals. The crowd claimed the apostles were wonder-workers. But instead of preaching miracles—or strategies for evangelism and global renewal—Peter and John continued to preach Jesus Christ, crucified and resurrected. Their message called their listeners to reality—to a true life found through repentance and belief in the work and person of Jesus Christ.

Repentance does not always result in external happiness, joy, and success, but it does bring a confidence that allows us to face and obey God's will through the grace received in Jesus Christ. Conversion also prompts a change of life-style, a new system of ethics, and often a painful death to sin. But confusing these joys or trials with the gospel can be devastating to even the serious believer. The gospel of experience will not keep us and deliver us on a life-long basis. When people who have become Christians for the benefits it will bring them make this discovery, they are prey to the zealous cults that promise better experiences and share greater testimonies.

The gospel, then, is based solely on the objective work of Jesus Christ. The great mystery of the faith is that Christ has died, Christ is risen, Christ will come again. The biblical pattern and model shows that we should preach Christ, not the gospel of varying results.

Foundation for Freedom

Christ's work in history frees us from comparative Christianity. It protects us from the sin of spiritual navel-gazing. In the church we can face sin, deal with it properly before God, and call for obedience. Faith in Christ gives us the Holy Spirit, who enables us with His power to face, work through, and grow in the midst of our problems. The gospel protects us from having always to look for that elusive "something more," which cults and other aberrant Christian groups unhesitatingly promise to the burdened believer.

3

The Lord Led Me

"The Lord led me."

"I felt led of the Lord."

Have you ever spoken or heard such phrases? What is your reaction to hearing them? Inwardly do you ever question their validity?

Many Christians are easily manipulated by anything that hints of spirituality. And who can be more spiritual than an enthusiastic member of a cult or other aberrant group?

In his book *Youth, Brainwashing and the Extremist Cults,* Ronald Enroth says, "Most cult groups display great skill in using biblical language and Christian terminology. Even Eastern religious cults appeal to the Bible for support and affirmation by a selective use of texts that fit their own systems."[1] Enroth adds, "Basic to the biblical view of God's adversary is the fact that he claims to be very religious."[2]

Mary Baker Eddy claimed to have new spiritual insights and used the Bible as the foundation for Christian Scientism. The Jehovah's Witnesses also use Scripture as their authority. Observe the extent of the spiritual appeal in the following letter written by Karen Layton, personal secretary to Jim Jones:

> Special blessings come to those who honor the work of God with their offerings. In recent meetings there has been a revelation about obedience offerings of certain amounts.... God will also reveal to Pastor Jones what your obedience offering should be.[3]

"But he was a manipulative cult leader," you say. Yes, but ask yourself how often you have said, "The Lord led me." It sounds spiritual, but nearly every cult touts this phrase or an equivalent.

When we as Evangelicals couple this phrase with a definition of spirituality based on frequency and fervor of devotions, quiet time, prayer, evangelism, and Bible study or sheer subjective emotion, we are wide open to manipulation and deception by groups that define spirituality in similar terms. We can easily become confused about who is spiritual and who isn't.

A Biblical Phrase?

We frequently fail to question and challenge leaders who present "new" spiritual insights or truths or who claim to be led by the Lord. Perhaps we fail to challenge our own use or misuse of the phrase, "The Lord led me."

In reality, God does lead us. God's direction is clearly evident throughout Scripture and history, throughout even our individual, private histories. However, "The Lord led me" can be a cover-up, disguising our own desires, irresponsibility, and attempts at manipulation. What an easy way to avoid responsibility for making the decisions continually placed before us! A misuse of this phrase can easily border on taking God's name in vain.

At first glance the phrase sounds quite spiritual, but a close examination of Scripture reveals that it is not always biblical. On several occasions the phrase is used by or to describe false prophets or deceptive people. Jacob deceived his father by spiritualizing issues. Esau, Jacob's brother, had just gone hunting. Too quickly, it seemed, Jacob, claiming to be Esau, brought the killed game to his father. "How did you find game so quickly?" Isaac asked. Having usurped Esau's place, Jacob lied to his sick, blind father. But notice Jacob's very "spiritual" response: "The Lord your God gave me success" (Genesis 27:20) .

Jacob was playing dangerous games, spiritualizing in order to manipulate someone he knew would believe such words. Jacob wasn't a false cult leader or prophet; he was God's own chosen servant.

The Gibeonites tried this same tactic of spiritual veneering on Joshua. Joshua and his army had destroyed the city of Ai, and the Gibeonites feared they were next. To deceive Joshua, they dressed up as if they had traveled from a far country. When they came face-to-face with Joshua, they spiritualized issues to manipulate him. "Joshua asked, 'Who are you and where do you come from?' They answered: 'Your servants have come from a very distant country because of the fame of the Lord your God'" (Joshua 9:8-9).

Joshua bit at their line baited with "spiritualese" and he was hooked. He immediately made a treaty with them. Joshua and Isaac, both leaders chosen by God, were deceived by spiritual talk.

Leaders were not the only biblical characters deceived by such language. Jeremiah
cried out God's displeasure with His people
who followed the ones blindly claiming, "Thus
saith the Lord."

> Then the Lord said to me, "The
> prophets are prophesying lies in my
> name.... (They are prophesying to
> you...delusions of their own
> minds" (Jeremiah 14:14).

> "I have heard what the prophets
> say who prophesy lies in my name.
> They say, 'I had a dream! I had a
> dream!'" (Jeremiah 23:25).

Time has not strengthened our Achilles'
heel. The deception of God's people by those
who "spiritualize" always has been and will be
with us. It sounds so right, yet the deception is
so subtle. We may not be using God as an
excuse for a lie, as was Jacob; we may simply
be deceiving ourselves, thinking God endorses
our own fabrications. For twelve years, I
served as the Dean of the Chapel at Gordon
College. It is located on the picturesque and
historic north shore of Boston—perhaps one of
the most scenic areas in the United States,

especially in the fall. One spring I received more than twenty letters from leaders of musical groups, pastors, and evangelists who had been "led by the Lord" to minister to the students during the first two weeks of October. Why, I wondered, doesn't God ever seem to lead ministries to New England during February? Either we should have cancelled classes for a week and held twenty chapel services, or the Holy Spirit was confused, or someone had bad hearing.

Almost all cult leaders and Christians who manipulate place a high emphasis on being "led by the Lord." When we misuse this term, we can easily make ourselves prey to cults or churches moving in controlling directions.

Stephen B. Clark describes in his book *Man and Woman in Christ* how some people justify their hidden agendas: "I am trying to be led by the Spirit, and the Spirit has not led me to adopt the kind of position that scripture seems to teach."[4]

This approach is not commonly represented in scholarly literature, but can be heard among Christians at large. You will notice that the "spiritual" is placed above the authority of Scripture. Clark states, "The statement...'led by the Spirit' can be a way to bypass scriptural authority. This happens when someone makes the Spirit's leading the decisive factor in accepting anything as true. When such people say they are 'waiting for the Spirit's leading,' they are saying that they personally require direct revelation or inspiration in order to accept something as true.... It would be a mistake, they feel, to pattern our lives on the way he was leading a group of Christians 2000 years ago. Such a position does not deny outright the authority of scripture, but it does amount to such a denial in practice."[5]

Charles Farah, Jr., of Oral Roberts University tells the story of a young Evangelical who carried this framework of thinking to its logical conclusion: "I don't read my Bible anymore," the young man said. "I don't have to read my Bible devotionally anymore, because I get mine direct."[6] This young man discovered no new tricks. He offered a clear picture of the sentiments of the false teachers who challenged both Old and New Testament leaders.

In the first century those who thought that personal revelation was an authority above Scriptures were called Gnostics. The idea is dispelled by Peter in his second letter: "Grace and peace be yours in abundance through the

knowledge of God and of Jesus our Lord"
(2 Peter 1:2).

Peter did not point to or single out some
Christian's superior leading. He addresses
all Christians as having real knowledge in
Christ. It is the same kind of holistic, non-
Gnostic knowledge to which Paul refers in
1 Corinthians 2:12, 14.[7]

We must ever guard ourselves against the
words and pet phrases that hint of superior
spirituality.

Open and Shut Doors

What Christian groups and other cults call
"the open-door policy" is another dangerous
veneer of spiritualization. Both sectors frequently refer to "God's shutting (or opening)
the door."

Right from the start, let me make my position clear. God does open and close doors. I
have seen evidence of this in my life, and I am
sure you have in yours. It is encouraging to
reflect on life and remember the times God has
indeed shut or opened doors. Such memories
build our faith. The danger, however, is to
view all lost opportunities as shut doors. The
convenient phrase "God closed the door" can
be a variation on the tune previously men-

tioned: manipulation, avoiding responsibility, and self-justification.

While I was speaking in the Southwest one time, a young Christian in deep distress asked me if we could discuss his job. It was clear that he had been irresponsible in establishing priorities, was undisciplined, and had been fired as a result. After a long discussion, he concluded, "I guess God must be shutting the door for me here."

I don't agree.

God does shut doors, of course. Since that discussion, however, I have been asking myself whether Christians use this phrase too freely. Do we use the phrase as a set of spiritual buzzwords to avoid responsibility or to cover up a fear of going through an open door of opportunity? Do we say "God has shut the door" when the lost opportunity is really a result of our own failure?

In Scripture, the closed-door policy is pictured in two ways. The Bible is full of accounts in which God closed doors to redirect the lives of people who trusted in Him. However, Scripture also couples the shut-door policy with the sin of neglect.

Remember the parable of the ten virgins? The story implies faith, morality, and virtue on the part of all ten virgins. But some were fool-ish. When the hour of the wedding arrived, they did not take the opportunity to provide suffi-cient fuel. In one moment the door shut and their opportunity passed (Matthew 25:1-13).

Their lack of oil was a result of doing noth-ing. Jesus attributed no serious evil or sin to them; they were simply indifferent to opportu-nities before them. They perceived a door shut because of neglect—just like the young man who lost his job. They followed the shut-door policy, and Christ labeled them foolish—not spiritually alert.

The use of the phrase "God shut the door" may reveal more about neglect than spirituali-ty. "How shall we escape if we ignore such a great salvation?" (Hebrews 2:3). "Do not for-get to entertain strangers.... Do not forget to do good and to share with others, for with such sacrifices God is pleased" (Hebrews 13:2,16).

White clapboard New England homes become dark, decaying buildings with time and neglect. Failure to put fuel in a jet will never get the plane or its passengers to the desired destination. We don't have to choose evil or willfully sin to spoil our character—neglect alone is sufficient.

Closed doors may be the result of good

things left undone. No evil was attributed to
the travelers who passed by the wounded man
on the road to Jericho; they simply passed by.
On Judgment Day there will be much talk of
"closed doors," but the meaning of the phrase
will then be different from our usual intent. It
will be used in regard to empty lamps, buried
talents, tasteless salt, and deeds left undone.

God's Word challenges us to walk through
the open doors set before us and to perform
good works. If a door is shut, we must not be
too quick to attribute the blockage to God. We
need to see all these easy-answer phrases in
their biblical context. Only when we see the
total picture are we protected from self-deception and a lopsided Christianity that is a dangerous cultic look-alike.

Night-shift Christianity

What is at the root of Christian groups who
spiritualize issues to justify their life-style and
service to God? Could it be a truncated view
of the work of the Holy Spirit?

We have limited the work of God's Spirit
to small aspects of our lives, those we term
"spiritual."

I once had a fascinating discussion with a
person whom God had placed in a strategic

position of international leadership. Decisions made by his company affected families, nations, and the needy worldwide. The man was a sincere Christian and exhibited an honest desire to live according to God's way. I was pleased that our conversation turned to spiritual matters, but I was puzzled when he said, "I admire men like you who have received a call into full-time Christian service. I have always wanted to be in full-time Christian work."

What a tragedy, I thought. He made such a distinction between my work and his. He saw "the ministry" as a higher calling than his own. He saw his job—and the jobs of others in the secular work place—as ordinary or perhaps God's second best.

The Bible presents life in a different perspective. All life is to be under the lordship of Christ. Every Christian's life is a ministry. Decisions made by this man's company had global impact. How unfortunate (and unbiblical) that he couldn't view the influence he had as an open door of opportunity to bring his total life under the lordship of Christ, as an open door to be used by God like Daniel in Babylon!

I have come to realize that this man is not

alone in his view of himself as a second-class Christian. Many Christians live under similar clouds of uselessness, feeling as though they are God's second best because they are not in "full-time" Christian work. Such feelings and the guilt that accompanies them make laypeople susceptible to cults and manipulators who solicit commitments to or promise opportunities for full-time service.

James and Marcia Rudin state, in their book *Prison or Paradise?*, "Cult followers often work full-time for the group. They work very long hours, for little or no pay."[8]

Most cults, like most Evangelicals, divide time and activities into two categories: the sacred and the secular. Michael Griffiths describes this situation: "Thus, part of our life is spent 'spiritually'—at innumerable meetings, in personal prayer and Bible reading, in public worship and in profitable' conversation with men about their souls. The rest of our time, however, must, perforce, be spent in a less worthy way on 'the things of this world'—eating, drinking, sleeping, working, playing, being with our families, digging in the garden, having holidays and so forth."[9]

We overlook the scriptural teaching that God has ordained all these "secular" activities and therefore must have some intention in them. Scripture regards everything we do as part of our Christian walk. Dividing existence into narrow, compact divisions dissolves the practical delights of a satisfied, effective, and fulfilled life in Jesus Christ. The instruction of Scripture is remarkably vivid and unclouded and cannot easily be spiritualized: "So whether you eat or drink or whatever you do, do it all for the glory of God" (I Corinthians 10:31).

Relaxation, for example, was an integral part of the spiritual life of Jesus Christ: "Then, because so many people were coming and going that they did not even have a chance to eat, he said to them, 'Come with me by yourselves to a quiet place and get some rest.' So they went away by themselves in a boat to a solitary place" (Mark 6:31-32).

Christ Negates Sin, Not Humanity

Christ came to negate sin, not our humanity. Jesus Christ seeks to redeem us from our sins, not from relaxation, work, fulfillment in life, and food consumption.

Paul echoes the theme of our humanness. He invites us to think about and examine all of life, not simply one "spiritual" division or one segment we label as "spirituality." "Finally, sisters and brothers, whatever is true, whatever is noble, whatever is right, whatever is pure, whatever is lovely, whatever is admirable—if anything is excellent or praiseworthy—think about such things.... And the God of peace will be with you" (Philippians, 4:8-9).

Paul does not insult our intelligence by telling us what is pure or by assigning purity to our "spiritual" compartment of life. Paul presents an expansive, wide-open invitation that activates our minds to be fully involved in the totality of life. The words *whatever* and *anything* invite us to discover all God has created. Sanctification is not the development of one spiritual aspect of reality; it involves doing everything, living every minute creatively and obediently to the glory of God.

In a personal letter to the Ephesians, Paul addresses various issues of life: talk, honest work, compassion, kindness, and warnings against drunkenness and debauchery. He then says that we are to be filled with God's Spirit (5:18). The Spirit does not influence our spiritual activities only. Paul speaks of relationships in the home. He encourages fairness between slaves and masters and responsible living in all our relationships.

The Book of Romans reveals an interesting

twist: "This is also why you pay taxes, for the authorities are God's servants, who give their full time to governing" (13:6). Paying our taxes is an act of spirituality.

In his book *Unsplitting Your Christian Life,* Michael Griffiths raises a noteworthy point concerning the affirmation given by God at the baptism of Christ. God said, "You are my Son whom I love; with you I am well pleased" (Luke 3:22). God made this statement to Jesus, a young man who had spent his whole life in a small village. Jesus had been working as a carpenter and living at home with His family. We are told little about those hidden years, but so much is suggested in one sentence: "Jesus grew in wisdom and stature, and in favor with God and men" (Luke 2:52). The point: God affirmed Christ in His humanity, and ministry followed.[9]

Christ's humanity was the central issue Satan attacked in the wilderness temptations. Jesus was challenged to prove His humanity by proving Himself spiritually. The challenge was repeated by the crowds at the foot of the cross: "Let him save himself if he is the Christ of God" (Luke 23:35). After all, spiritual people shouldn't bleed, suffer, or hurt.

Many Christians who fight for the doctrine

of creation often deny it by compartmentaliz-
ing life into that which is spiritual and that
which is secular. At this point they slip across
the border and into the heresy of many cults.
Michael Griffiths elaborates on some of the
effects of this way of thinking: "It is because
of this kind of 'compartmentalization' that
Hosea rebukes Ephraim.... Israel had plenty
of religion, plenty of sacrifices and burnt offer-
ings; but the Lord values mercy towards men
and knowledge of Himself more highly than
those."[10] The Hebrews of Hosea's day had
problems applying spirituality to all of life (see
Hosea 6:6; 7:8). Griffiths goes on,

> If we adopt this division of life into
> sacred and secular, then it must fol-
> low that the more time we spend on
> "spiritual things," the more holy we
> shall be. Is it not true that for some
> reason we tend to regard the voca-
> tion of the Christian minister or
> overseas missionary as being a cut
> above that of the ordinary run of
> believers? We instinctively feel, no
> doubt, that he can spend more time
> saying his prayers and reading his
> Bible. The common expression

"He's in full-time Christian work"
simply reeks of the idea that the
work of some Christians is intrinsi-
cally more Christian than that of
others.... All Christians, whatever
their employment, are full-time
Christian workers. If we do not
maintain this, we shall be in danger
of having a caste system within the
Church, a ruling hierarchy who lord
it over their humbler brethren.[11]

Toward a Spiritual Vocation

Do you ever feel like a second-class
Christian? No one needs to. Through Paul,
God affirms all vocations as spiritual work.
"Brothers, each man, as responsible to God,
should remain in the situation God called him
to" (I Corinthians 7:24). The surrounding
verses make it clear that Paul is referring to situations such as marriage, national and racial
customs, and various professions. All roles
are ordained and affirmed as called in Christ.

When we Christians compartmentalize life,
we step frighteningly close to the world of
the cults. God calls us to live every moment
creatively before Jesus Christ and under His
lordship.

Some might say, "But doesn't Paul elsewhere say we are to place our minds on higher
things, to set our 'hearts on things above'?"

Yes, but Paul's statement, in Colossians 3:1-
2, is not a call to deny reality; it is placed within the context of God's grace revealed in Jesus
Christ. Because Christ is now with God, we
must focus our minds on Christ. He will free
us from guilt so that we can live each day fully
and to the glory of God. This is the foundation
of self-acceptance, self-esteem, and service to
others. Immediately after issuing the call to
place our minds on higher things, Paul says,
"Whatever you do, whether in word or deed,
do it all in the name of the Lord Jesus, giving
thanks to God the Father through him"
(Colossians 3:17).

Paul then fleshes out the implications of this
mind-set. He encourages fathers not to embit-
ter children, lest they become discouraged. He
encourages slaves to obey their masters. Why?
To gain spiritual "brownie points"? No.
Because life should be a service to God. Life
itself is full-time Christian work. Later in the
same chapter of Colossians (just in case his
readers misunderstood), Paul repeats himself,
saying, "Whatever you do, work at it with all
your heart working for the Lord, not for men"

(3:23). Yes, the *whatevers* refer to prayer, Bible study, worship, witnessing, and helping the poor, but they also include every other aspect of our humanity.

Scripture begins with Creation and climaxes with Christ redeeming all of life (Romans 8:22-23). The Bible, from the Creation to the final redemption, portrays life as a unity. We are called to be integrated, healthy people devoted to serving God, believers living every minute—with our families, at work, in prayer, and even paying taxes—before God. All facets of life are integral parts of God's will on this earth.

God does lead. God does call people. God does open and close doors. God does direct people to work full-time in missionary work and on the church staff. But God is not limited to working only in the spheres of life that we spiritualize. When we divide life into snug "spiritual" and "nonspiritual" compartments, we are thinking heretically and may blindly accept a cultic view of life. Without realizing where we are heading, we may cause ourselves or our children to spiritualize things, to validate what God has already ordained as good. Or, on the other hand, we may be in danger of using God's name in vain to justify our irresponsibility, manipulation of others, and spiritual pride. Categorizing time and actions will not only create guilt, but also make us vulnerable to cult leaders who speak our own spiritual language deceptively to move us spiritually to a wrong commitment.

4

They Even Share
Their Burdens and
Pray Together

Both Christians and cult members place high spiritual value on group sharing. In both circles, the foundation for community life and growth is the discussion of personal sins, problems, and intimacies. Christians emphasize prayer for each other's problems, but many do not know the hidden hazards involved.

I have met Christians who, during the high emotional pitch of a church or group prayer meeting, have shared intimate details of their lives—and for years afterward have regretted the tormenting results of their admission. A fine line exists between healthy openness and destructive control and manipulation.

Consider the following questions:

— Do any scriptural limitations protect us from the liabilities of sharing our problems with others?
— Is burden-sharing a sign of true spiritual maturity?
— Since both Christians and cult members place value on group prayer for problems, how do we protect ourselves from stepping over the line that separates us?
— Are there innate dangers in sharing intimacies?
— How much should we tell, and to whom should we tell it?
— Does God ask that everything be told?
— Does a church, fellowship group, friend, or pastor have the right to pressure us into sharing intimate secrets?
— What are the biblical guidelines?

When sharing problems, difficulties, and burdens becomes a sign of spirituality, the door to manipulation, exploitation, and other unhealthy group dynamics is unlatched.

Might we elevate one truth of Scripture and give it much higher value than does Scripture? During the seventies I visited a church in California that centered around sharing and praying for personal problems—an emphasis with which I concur. But I quickly noticed that the emphasis in this congregation left little room for victories or for ordinary good days. Such a premium was set on "struggling" that one felt spiritually inferior if he or she wasn't always routing problems. My friendships with people in this congregation became difficult as I always felt the pressure to share bearing down on every conversation. We couldn't go out to eat, attend a concert, or go to the beach without spending some wrenching time sharing our struggles.

When pushed to its limit, this subtle pressure to share our struggles can lead to sessions in which people are forced to "confess" wrongs they never committed or thoughts that never entered their minds. In some groups it's not acceptable to "pass" when you feel no particular trouble haunting you.

The following three accounts tell of various group-sharing sessions. The first is from the Congressional Record of May 15, 1981, and it describes Jonestown; the other two are from an article on an Evangelical fellowship based in New England, published in *Boston* magazine.

> As a complement to the physical pressures, he [Jim Jones] exerted mental pressures on his follow-

ers.... [Tactics included] so-called "struggle meetings" or catharsis sessions in which recalcitrant members were interrogated, required to confess their "wrong-doing," and then punished with alternate harshness and leniency.[1]

—

"Community adults would decide what my sin was, then just lay into me," she recalled. "I wasn't allowed to speak to my father when he phoned; they told me it was the Lord's will that I not speak with him.... The way I was making beds looked 'rebellious' to them, so I was assigned to scrub the bathrooms. Each day I'd get yelled at and forced to scrub them again."[2]

—

"They pushed me into saying I lusted after my little daughter," said Brad Mason [not his real name]. "Their idea was that only when you recognize your total depravity can you let Jesus go to work."[3]

In this age of religious and spiritual confusion, it is important to examine biblical attitudes and guidelines for discussing intimacies, problems, and secret sins with pastors, friends, fellowship groups, and prayer groups.

Exploitation and manipulation in this regard can be very subtle and spiritual-sounding. One short conversation with a minister opened my eyes to this deception. I was having an excellent day—one of the best in several months. My minister friend asked, "How is it going?"

"Fine," I responded.

But that wasn't what he wanted to hear. He placed his hand on my shoulder and asked, "How is it really going?"

Suddenly I felt guilty, as though something were wrong with having a good day. A little later he commented, "Your cold is getting to you, isn't it?" It really wasn't, but I began to wonder what I was projecting.

The misuse and exploitation of basic counseling skills, which should be reserved for formal counseling sessions, can place others in a vulnerable position. It can make them dependent on our support, concern, and spiritual parenting. Many pastors and leaders are experts at playing this game of one-upmanship. It can be a subtle tool that forces others to pay homage to our insights and concerns for them. Many people assume that leaders or other Christians know more about them than they do about themselves. When this assumption is encouraged through the subtle misuse of counseling skills, we are fair game for exploitation.

Christ modeled for us the importance of selectively discussing and revealing personal struggles. Did you ever wonder how disciples like Matthew knew about the temptations of Jesus Christ? Christ obviously told His close friends about these deep struggles and difficulties.

Scripture calls us to confess our faults, sins, and problems to God and to each other. Yet all the guidelines of Scripture warn us to remember that, in all relationships, we are the guardians of each other's vulnerabilities. This is spelled out clearly and practically.

Coming Out of the Closet

The last quarter of the twentieth century may go down in history as the age when everyone "came out of the closet." Our society and culture encourage people to "let it all hang out," to "tell all." Is this also the call for the believer?

Christ had something to say about "coming out of the closet" when He taught the disciples about prayer: "When you pray, go into your room ["closet," KJV], close the door and pray to your Father, who is unseen. Then your Father, who sees what is done in secret, will reward you" (Matthew 6:6).

Following this instruction, Jesus taught them how to pray publicly. He emphatically pointed out that not everything should be taken out of the closet. Jesus Christ protects our privacy.

Cults and some encounter groups are not the only parties guilty of negating privacy; some Christians pressure people under the guise of spirituality. Such disregard for privacy is the spirit of our age. This exploitation is the infection of our generations.

Christ's words are the antibiotic that will fight against the infection of personal exploitation.

Paul reiterates Christ's position. Although he tells us to speak the truth in love (Ephesians 4:15), he doesn't encourage us to tell everything. Speaking the truth in love does not mean having a cathartic session. Paul himself didn't spill all. To Timothy he wrote, "Here is a trustworthy saying that deserves full acceptance: Christ Jesus came into the world to save sinners—of whom I am the worst" (I Timothy 1:15).

When referring to his sin, Paul used the

present tense, saying he was currently in need of God's grace. Note that Paul never told what his secret sins were, the nature of them, or his weaknesses. He spoke truthfully, but he didn't list all the details. Paul guarded his own vulnerability. This basic principle will also protect us from those who might seek to exploit our frailties and make us codependent on them. Secret sins are to be dealt with secretly. We have the freedom and are encouraged to keep some confessions between ourselves and God. It is important for us to respect others' decisions not to discuss personal inner struggles. Christ discussed His own temptations of His own free will.

Who Hears What?

Scripture protects not only our personal privacy but also the privacy of others. Sins against another person are to be discussed only with that person and with careful consideration for that person's vulnerabilities. If the issues cannot be resolved personally, only then should the problem be brought before mediators.

"If your brother sins against you, go and show him his fault, just between the two of you. If he listens to you, you have won your brother over. But if he will not listen, take one or two others along, so that "every matter may be established by the testimony of two or three witnesses. If he refuses to listen to them, tell it to the church; and if he refuses to listen even to the church, treat him as you would a pagan or a tax collector" (Matthew 18:15-17).

This passage leads us to protect relationships, seek reconciliation, maintain respect, and guard each other's weaknesses. When we are wronged by someone, God calls us to contact that person individually, not the congregation or another friend. Jesus asks us to walk down a private road, not a public thoroughfare. He asks us to fight our own battles, not to drag others in to join our defense or our offense. Again, privacy seems to be the biblical standard for the handling of problems.

If difficulties arise within a group or sins are committed against a group or community, the scriptural model calls for dealing with the problem in the group. Paul publicly challenged Peter in Antioch when he followed Galatians into legalistic enslavement (see Galatians 2:11 and Acts 15). His example can serve as a guideline for group confrontation and submission.

We must always return to a biblical base to

guard us against the potential abuse of "community." Christian groups and cults that misuse or exploit the sharing of problems reverse the scriptural order; they emphasize confessing private issues publicly, confessing their neighbor's faults one to another, and secretly taking to God those issues that should be openly confronted.

There's no getting around it: Sin that we do not face will ultimately destroy us. When we are isolated by sin, we are most vulnerable to guilt and exploitation by other people. God has given us practical guidelines for our own benefit and growth. When we discuss others' problems with third parties, we magnify the problems, for we become a part of them. The circle of confidence in our lives should only be as wide as the sin committed. Unless we are willing to facilitate the solution, we become part of the problem.

Learning these basic protective principles will prevent us from doing all the right things in the wrong way. How easy for us to get turned around! It is exactly what happened to Judas Iscariot. After he betrayed Jesus, Judas was sorry for his sins. He confessed them; he was penitent; he even returned the blood money. Sadly, Judas did all the right things in the wrong way. Confession was not enough. He confessed his sins to the high priest and elders rather than to God. As a result he felt no resolution, no release of guilt, and he ultimately destroyed himself. Could it be that many of those who died in Jonestown were doing all the right things—in the wrong way?

Knowing Ourselves First

Paul wrote to the church in Ephesus and urged them "to live a life worthy of the calling you have received" (Ephesians 4:1). Then Paul defined the various characteristics of the calling: "Be completely humble and gentle; be patient, bearing with one another in love. Make every effort to keep the unity of the Spirit through the bond of peace" (4:2-3).

Notice the imperative of the last statement: "Make every effort...." In any community, quality relationships do not automatically happen. Because we live in a fallen world, deterioration is the normal process of events. God calls us to be diligent in developing our own character and meaningful, trusting relationships with others. A church's unity of the Spirit is not created through meetings, activities, programs, or pastors. Within this context, unity has been established by God in Christ. We are merely caretakers, called to nourish, guard, protect, and maintain this unity through the bond of peace. Scripture does not picture peace as an absence of conflict, but as confidence in God's sovereign hand in the midst of conflict. The bond of peace is made strong by five qualities, like five strands of rope: humbleness, gentleness, patience, forbearance, and love.

When we are humble of mind, we recognize ourselves for who we are. We realistically face our strengths, weaknesses, and limitations. I make a point of separating limitations from weaknesses. Many Christians and cult members confuse limitations with sin. But limitations are the marks of our humanity. Even before the Fall, man and woman were limited in their abilities and knowledge. They were not—we are not—God. Limitations are the marks of the created. Weaknesses, however, are those sins and emotional difficulties that have resulted from living in a fallen and fractured world.

When we become aware of God's grace, patience, and gentleness in dealing with our limitations and weaknesses, we can start being patient with others. Gentleness and patience develop in the context of humbleness of mind.

When we are aware of and sensitive toward our own clay feet, we are best able to be sensitive to and guardians of the vulnerabilities of our fellow believers.

Suffer With One Another

The Greek *anechomai*, commonly translated *forbearance*, is used fifteen times in the New Testament. It means "to put up with, to tolerate, to suffer with the weaknesses of each other's personalities." Can God mean that we are to suffer with each other's temperaments, dispositions, and brokenness?

Paul understood that our personalities are always with us. A community maintains the unity given by God's grace when its members tolerate, put up with, and suffer with each other, not when they build expectations of perfection. How can we tolerate and suffer with other believers, when we cannot tolerate our own temperaments? God in His grace points us down a road of humility.

Most of us do not enjoy being hemmed in by the givens of our personalities. We can give ourselves emotional claustrophobia. Because we are created in the image of God, we are brimful of mystery and complexity. On top of that add the many consequences of the

Fall, sin, mixed motives, genetic and personality weaknesses, and we are asked to put up with a lot. Keep in mind that the compulsive person in your church or fellowship may not relish the time he or she spends organizing and reorganizing. The absentminded person is often embarrassed when he or she walks in late. Not all behavior that appears to be antisocial is passive aggression. When the givens of our personalities surface, we wish we could acquire the best qualities of everyone we know. "Why can't I be like so-and-so? More organized? A better provider? More positive? More successful?" Or, instead of being intolerant of ourselves, we might turn our demand for perfection outward, toward others, and say, "Why can't my pastor be like that pastor? My partner like that person? My children more like the children of others?" These high expectations make us vulnerable to leaders who promise easy, formula solutions for minimizing the complexities of individual and community life.

Making Others in Our Image

Paul encourages us to forbear each other in love. In the stage musical *My Fair Lady*, Henry Higgins asked, "Why can't a woman be more like a man? Why can't a woman be like me?" We all have our own preludes and fugues developed on this same theme. We may not, like Higgins, sing the tunes aloud, but how often do we repeat the sentiment in attitude, action, and body language?

Do the following words sound familiar? "I love you so much that I am going to relieve you of the burden of your personality. I am now enlightened, and it is my responsibility to follow God's guidance and create you in my own image." When Christians demand of each other identical life-styles and stifling conformity, they create an environment of unhealthy loyalty that can easily be shifted to a destructive group. Cults want to create followers into given images set by the group or its leaders. We become vulnerable to this when we confuse compatibility with sameness, and unity with uniformity. Forbearance assumes diversity. When the standard is conformity, what is the need for tolerance, for "putting up with" each other, for wearing patience and gentleness?

Paul calls us to be diverse in our relationships and to minister to each other the gospel of peace. Christians are called to help others be at peace with who they are.

Learn to Say "No"

Because we live in a fallen world, people—
even Christians—may try to manipulate us. In
such situations we must know how to say "no"
without feeling guilty. We must look to the
Scriptures for guidelines that will help us discern: When should we say "no," and when are
we required to go the second mile? Many burdens and problems presented to us are legitimate, but others are not. God's wisdom in
dealing with the burdens of a group far sur-
passes our own. Paul elaborates on this issue
in his letter to the Galatians:

> Carry each other's burdens, and in
> this way you will fulfill the law of
> Christ. If anyone thinks he is
> something when he is nothing, he
> deceives himself. Each man should
> test his own actions. Then he can
> take pride in himself, without com-
> paring himself to somebody else,
> for each one should carry his own
> load (6:2-6).

Notice the checks and balances that protect
both parties. Each person is responsible for
carrying his or her own burdens. We are not to

drop ours at someone else's feet and expect that he or she will carry them, but we are to carry the burden of others. Scripture does not ask us to remove other people's burdens from them. It asks that we bear them. God does not call us to snatch away from others their burdens, because when we carry our own burdens, we grow. If we take away someone's difficulties, we make them overdependent on us. The goal of the Christian life is dependency on God. Any dependency short of that makes us open to deception and manipulation.

In this fallen world we are subject to the heavy weights of ill health, aging, and unexpected tragedies. We must not feel guilty for sharing exceptional legitimate needs, for bringing our burdens to the attention of other Christians. We should not feel guilty when our circumstances allow others the opportunity to serve, care, grow, and love.

Bringing a burden to others is being willing to confess needs and acknowledge that life has laid on us burdens that we cannot carry alone. Being a burden involves climbing into another person's arms and letting him or her carry both us and the burden.

Paul goes on to place this instruction in the context of encouragement: "Therefore, as we have opportunity, let us do good to all people, especially to those who belong to the family of believers" (Galatians 6:10). We will not always have our parents, partners, children, or material possessions. Someday all of the gifts of this life will be stripped away. Paul encourages us to serve each other in the midst of forbearance or tolerance.

On occasion, friends or colleagues may call on us to be their lightning rod—to receive and soak up the shock of their burdens. To be effective and not destroyed in the process, a lightning rod must be grounded. When taking this role, we need to be grounded in humbleness of mind, patience, gentleness, prayer, and God's Word. Only then can we absorb the shock in a godly way.

5

But We Have a New Testament Church

Many cults, as with numerous Christian groups, present themselves as being modeled after the New Testament church.

We all long and search for the "ideal" Christian community. We all have high expectations of the model Christian church. As Christians we esteem the New Testament church as our foundation and its fellowship as the goal for our community life. But beware. These expectations can make us unbiblically close to many cults who claim to be "the only true church since Bible times."

Often people boast that their home churches are patterned after the first-century church described in the New Testament. With stars in their eyes they tell of their congregations' thrilling impact and the evidence of God's blessing upon them. I do not deny their claims, but they frequently forget that the New Testament church was constantly beset with doctrinal, behavioral, even racial problems.

The Corinthians, for example, tolerated sexual aberration, misunderstood the resurrection of the dead, and misused the gifts of the Spirit, and some even got drunk at Communion services. The Galatians misrepresented the gospel and turned to legalism. The church in Colosse mixed Christian teachings with pagan worldviews.

Before we boast too loudly of being another New Testament church, we should reread Scripture carefully and comprehensively. The fragile first-century church needed constant apostolic instruction, guidance, confrontation, and direction. Can we expect more from our "New Testament church"? Many cults describe themselves as ideal communities; they promise perfect fellowship. Our yearning and search for such an ideal can quickly turn our heads in the direction of those who offer something beyond what God is committed to establish in the here and now with human beings, who are both fallen and redeemed.

Dietrich Bonhoeffer saw this problem creeping into the German church before the establishment of the Third Reich. He wrote,

> God hates visionary dreaming; it makes the dreamer proud and pretentious. The man who fashions a visionary ideal of community demands that it be realized by God, by others, and by himself. He enters the community of Christians with his demands, sets up his own law, and judges the brethren and God Himself accordingly. He stands adamant a living reproach to all others in the circle of brethren. He acts as if he is the creator of the Christian community, as if his dream binds men together. When things do not go his way, he calls the effort a failure. When his ideal picture is destroyed, he sees the community going to smash. So he becomes, first an accuser of his brethren, then an accuser of God, and finally the despairing accuser of himself.[1]

What do you think of when you envision

fellowship? I often hear Christians saying, "There is no real fellowship in my church. I wish we had fellowship like they did in the New Testament church." You have probably heard and perhaps said something like, "I sure wish I belonged to another church, where there is deeper fellowship."

Let's be honest. How often do we think of fellowship in terms of nice people and what they can do to make us feel better, more comfortable, or more fulfilled? Our modern misunderstanding of fellowship is complicated by "me-first" messages presented in the religious media, which picture the church as the cosmic supermarket, a consumerist field day. We come to God with our spiritual credit cards to receive, on demand, all the displayed benefits. This system requires, however, no down payments, no installments, no responsibilities, just an I.D. We give nothing and in return receive warm feelings and participate in innumerable exciting activities. "Let's see. What would I like today?" What are the biblical definitions of fellowship? You may be surprised to find that fellowship in the New Testament is not equated with human-centered warmth or satisfying activities. Fellowship can never be created by us, only by God.

The apostle John states that true fellowship is found first in an understanding of God's grace.

> That which was from the beginning, which we have heard, which we have seen with our eyes, which we have looked at and our hands have touched—this we proclaim concerning the Word of life. The life appeared; we have seen it and testify to it, and we proclaim to you the eternal life, which was with the Father and has appeared to us. We proclaim to you what we have seen and heard, so that you also may have fellowship with us. And our fellowship is with the Father and with his Son, Jesus Christ. We write this to make our joy complete (I John 1:1-4).

John points out that Christian fellowship is based on an orthodox understanding of the person and work of Jesus Christ. Out of our knowledge of Christ comes our joy.

I once taught that we break fellowship with God every time we sin. I can remember hearing church conference speakers say that sin hinders fellowship. If that is true, the logical way to maintain fellowship with God and others is to refrain from sin. God hates sin, and I agree that we are to turn our backs on it. But if lack of sin is the criterion for a Christian's fellowship with God and others, what a precarious and dangerous tightrope we walk. We are left with no security. No wonder the cults are growing!

The Bible really gives us a much broad hope.

> This is the message we have heard from him and declare to you. God is light; in him there is no darkness at all. If we claim to have fellowship with him yet walk in the darkness, we lie and do not live by the truth. But if we walk in the light, as he is in the light, we have fellowship with one another, and the blood of Jesus, his Son, purifies us from all sin.

> If we claim to be without sin, we deceive ourselves and the truth is not in us. If we confess our sins, he is faithful and just and will forgive us our sins and purify us from all unrighteousness. If we claim we have not sinned, we make him out

to be a liar and his word has no
place in our lives (I John 1:5-10).

The key to fellowship with God is the work
of Jesus Christ through which we repent and
receive the grace and mercy of God.
Fellowship grows as we walk in the light.

John uses some serious words: deceive; lie;
God's word is not in us; we make God a liar.
Consider what he says about walking in darkness as opposed to walking in light. If we live
in darkness, we live in deception. If we live in
deception, we live in unreality. If we live in
unreality, we make God a liar. By contrast, if
we live in the light, we are continually cleansed
by Christ's blood.

Within this context John says that if we live
or act as if we do not have sin, we are walking
in darkness—and that is deception. If, on the
other hand, we walk in the light, we have fellowship with God. If sin kept us from fellowship, then we would never have fellowship!

A friend once admitted to me that he had
not sinned in more than three years. He had
"found the secret," he claimed. He had resist-
ed all temptation and continually "practiced
the presence of God." He obviously didn't
consider spiritual pride a sin. John clearly

states that when we claim we have no sin, we walk in darkness.

Many cults dangle the sin-free life in front of prospective members, but many Christians mistakenly reach for and expect the same prize.

Now, John says that if we walk in the light, we have fellowship. But if this does not mean living sinlessly, what does it mean? The sin we can be freed of is the sin of denying our sins.

Merely acknowledging reality. Have you ever walked into the playroom of a five-year-old in pitch darkness? You are taking your life in your hands! However, when you turn the light switch, you see what looks like the aftermath of a tornado. When the light is on, you watch your step; you are careful not to trip; you bend over to start cleaning up the disaster area and put the room in reasonable order. Light exposes reality and displays facts. Light reveals things as they are.

Notice John's use of the action verb walk. Walking assumes the ability to move, make decisions, be aware of directions, and initiate choices. If we walk in God's light, we see facts as they are and we choose to deal with them. Light reveals our sin.

Does Sin Hinder Fellowship?

As a child I was taught that walking in the light spiritually involved walking in sinless perfection. As long as my life was free from sin, I was walking in the light. In studying Scripture further, I have been forced to challenge this teaching as unbiblical and basically cultic. This view of the Christian walk says that if one thinks about immorality, bitterness, resentment, or exaggeration then suddenly he or she is in darkness: "Oh, now I have to breathe out a confession, so I can return to the light.... Wow! I am perfect again.... Whoops! Thought a bad thought; now I am out of fellowship again." This kind of thinking easily leads to schizophrenic behavior and deception in our fellowship with God and others.

According to John, walking in the light includes living with our sin and acknowledging our brokenness, vulnerability, and difficulties. Walking in the light enables us to be honest, protects us from spiritual pride, and most importantly, protects us from those cults that offer a perfect spirituality. Light reveals reality.

Darkness denies or covers up facts. It causes us to trip over the unseen mess in our hearts. Living in darkness will cause us to inflict pain on ourselves and others

Fellowship is not just having a good time, feeling good, smiling, and sharing spiritual excitement. Fellowship grows when we keep on walking in the light.

Darkness is pretending. Jesus said, "Men loved darkness instead of light because their deeds were evil" (John 3:19). Darkness hides their impure motives, their manipulations, and their transgressions.

John develops his theme by introducing an order of events that runs contrary to much contemporary teaching. He places fellowship between walking and confessing, then he concludes his list with cleansing. Many—myself included—would prefer to change the order so that it reads: walk, confess, be cleansed, and then have fellowship. Such a revised process seems much safer! It would protect us so we could hide our own sinfulness, deal with it in isolation, and then exclaim to anyone who would hear, "Isn't fellowship wonderful!" Walking in darkness, denying reality, allows us the luxury of risking little. But those who risk little gain little. Those who project spiritual perfection, like the Pharisees and some cult members, are shielded from spiritual growth.

Have you ever met a spiritually perfect person? Did you view him or her as living on a higher plane than yourself? Did you assume that person was sinless? If so, you are standing on dangerous ground. In his writings John establishes that God's grace in Christ frees us to trust the presence of God; we do not have to discover the spiritual gymnastic program that will allow us to practice the presence of God. God is present with us in all circumstances. Christ's light continually illuminates sin, which, if we confess, His grace continually cleanses.

Fellowship is facing sin, obeying God's Word, learning, praying with, growing alongside, and serving others. The whole of life is the arena in which we share fellowship together.

The church is called to reveal Jesus Christ to each other and to the world by living together in reality, honesty, and love. We are not called to witness to spiritual perfection, but to our need for God's daily grace.

With whom did Jesus have the greatest difficulty in this matter? The Pharisees, whom He called "hypocrites" (Matthew 23:15). The Greeks originated the word to denote an actor, one who played a role. To Jesus, the Pharisees' spiritual life was a colossal theater production.

Jesus Christ cannot give us growth or help us to be obedient if we act out a part—if we walk in darkness.

John was writing to believers, not to unbelievers. When we see and feel guilt over problems, secret sins, and struggles, we should rejoice. God is at work in our lives. The light has been turned on. God loves us and wants to help us clean up the mess.

What is darkness? Boasting of our spiritual maturity and perfection, playing a part that hides our true humanity.

John helps us to see and understand the nature of God's light so we won't spiritually trip up and sin. Note how he continues: "My dear children, I write this to you so that you will not sin" (1 John 2:1).

Quality fellowship begins here. The foundation for healthy Christian fellowship is not attending activities and sharing warm feelings, but walking in light.

Walking in Light Can Hurt Too

Once when I was in upstate New York for a conference, I took my children on a tour of a vineyard. The guide pointed out that every vine is cut back during the coldest weeks of January. If this isn't done, the more productive plants "take over" and smother the others, eventually reducing the quality of the overall crop. Such cut-back plants have long life spans. The ones left unpruned eventually stop producing quality grapes and die prematurely. The guide also noted that until a vine is seven years old, its grapes are not made into wine; only after years of pruning and patience does a crop reach its full sugar potential. During those first seven summers and winters the roots grow deep, becoming less and less vulnerable to root diseases. They intertwine with the root systems of other plants, and together they hold onto the nourishing topsoil.

Jesus reminds us that the Vinekeeper cuts back all the plants. Often Christians take new converts and immediately hold them up as spiritual trophies. Upon conversion, a black activist of the sixties was placed in a position of authority and leadership; he soon started a church that had cultic leanings. Could the Evangelical community have prevented his waywardness if they had allowed God time to make him strong, his roots deep, and his fruit mature?

God is not in a hurry. He deemed Moses ready to lead His people only after eighty years of training. Jesus was thirty when He started His public ministry. Paul spent the first few years of his Christian life in solitude and isolation. If we walk in the light, we will be pruned by the Vinekeeper. Being pruned involves facing sin. If we walk in the light, we will produce quality fruit, which only comes with time and the slow but sure development that accompanies it.

Too often our impatience with God, ourselves, and others gets us into trouble. We want perfection; we want fault-free fellowship; we want the promised utopian community now. But we, along with the rest of creation, groan for our final redemption. We are in the growing stage.

A Part of the Body

Our confused expectations of fellowship and our insistence on rapid-growth Christianity, coupled with our independent attitudes, contribute to our susceptibility to cults. Many churches have been established in reaction to liberalism or as an offshoot of a church that didn't seem to offer adequate fellowship. In cases where believers from such reactionary churches possess a shallow tradition and lack the authority a time-honored tradition brings, they are extremely vulnerable to the whims of a leader who might move them in a destructive direction.

Our countryside is dotted with independent cults as well as "independent" Bible churches, apostolic assemblies, and fellowship groups. If you are part of an independent church, you need to ask some serious questions in light of Scripture. From whom are you independent— from God? From Christ? From the rest of the body of Christ? Can the arm say, "I have no need of the foot"? Are you finding your identity in opposition to another Christian group? Can you be faithful to Scripture and cut yourself off from the rest of the body?

Both independent Christians and cults tend to confuse unity with uniformity. They tend to produce clones. But they are not alone. Many of us stand on old traditions associate only with our own kind—Charismatics with Charismatics, Baptists with Baptists, Presbyterians with Presbyterians, Nazarenes with Nazarenes. We seek out those who will reinforce our own likes and dislikes. How quickly we can grow blind to the rich diversity God has built into the body of Christ! How quickly we can grow blind to our own sin of writing off or discounting other members of the body of Christ! Such blindness brings with it a warm security, an assurance that we are the body. It allows us to identify ourselves in opposition to, rather than as a part of, a larger group. By remote control it removes from us our responsibility to "love one another" (John 13:35).

All cults view themselves as being independent; they identify themselves in opposition to other bodies. When independent attitudes are coupled with a misunderstanding of the believers' walk in the light, Christians are easy prey to a community that eternally promises "something better."

Again, Evangelicals are seldom drawn into a cult because they agree with the cult's doctrine. Rather it often happens because they see and want signs of great "spirituality." We must always keep before us John's discussion of walking in the light. We are not called to have great faith in God, but to have faith in a great God.

6

You Just Have to Hear Our Pastor!

"**Y**ou just have to hear our pastor!"

Sound familiar? I sometimes get the feeling Christians are more excited about their pastors than about Jesus Christ. Take the time to evaluate your expectations of your pastor. Do you expect an eternal flow of new, great wisdom, always presented with a flair? Do you build up unbiblical, superhuman expectations of leadership?

Occasionally I receive job descriptions from churches in search of a pastor. Sometimes their expectations are so absurd, they might as well require that the new pastor take yearly mission trips to Africa—without the aid of a boat or a plane.

A church in the Boston area called a new pastor. On the first Sunday evening he asked each member to write down what he or she considered the eight most important duties of an ideal pastor. He asked them to enumerate next to each item how many hours per week the pastor should give to this activity. Later he added up the largest number of hours expected for each category. The final tally showed that the ideal pastor was expected to spend 22 hours a week visiting; 18 hours studying; 20 hours counseling; 15 hours administering; 15 hours preparing and leading services; 4 hours attending community activities; 10 hours evangelizing, and 2 hours meeting with other local clergy. Total: 106 hours of work per week. Unfortunately they forgot such necessities as rest, sleep, prayer, eating, family relationships, home maintenance, and recreation. Any pastor who fulfills all a church's expectations risks functioning like a cult leader. Both Evangelicals and cult members seem to need and want an authority figure with charisma to meet their expectations.

Not long ago two strong Evangelical churches, one in the East and the other in the Southwest, applied for loans that would allow them to build new sanctuaries. The banks granted the loans on the condition that the pastor contractually agree to stay for an extended period of time. In both situations the bank felt the congregation was built around and held together by the personality of the senior pastor.

What an indictment of the direction of many Evangelical churches! This is not an issue unique to local congregations. Almost every major, successful, contemporary parachurch ministry is built around a single personality, who is able to attract a coterie of dedicated followers.

These followers tend to place on their leaders unbelievable pressure to perform. Such pressure opens the door to misuse of power, unhealthy dependency, and discouragement. In her excellent book *They Cry, Too!* Lucille Lavender points out how our expectations can create overwhelming grief and pain to those who minister.[1] In self-protection a leader can easily give in to the unrealistic and unbiblical demands placed upon him or her. These expectations can force pastors to play roles that run counter to biblical priorities. Unfortunately, these roles are also played by cult leaders: Cults offer the ideal leaders who lead the ideal communities.

A certain visitor to a Christian college

campus delivered a chapel sermon that was profound, biblical, and challenging, but his style was slow, deliberate, and low-key. Many students who had been raised in strongly Evangelical churches complained that the message lacked spiritual vitality. These students immediately rejected the solid content because it didn't sound "anointed" or "Spirit-led."

Several weeks later another speaker visited campus. His message contained little Scripture; a majority of the message criticized Evangelicals, social activists, the middle class, suburban life, Western culture, and various Christian organizations. Little in the sermon was biblically instructive or helpful in preparing the students for service, ministry, or growth. The sermon was punctuated with emotionally moving stories. At the end of the presentation, the speaker was given a standing ovation.

Sometime later I asked the same students who had thought the first speaker "unspiritual" what they thought of the second. There was little disagreement: He was definitely a man of God. It was apparent that none could remember the content of his talk, but they all felt he must have been led by God. "I felt God's holy presence, and I was challenged to commitment," one student said typically. For the first time I saw and understood how vulnerable people are in the presence of forceful leaders—leaders who communicate with a flair.

This is just a minor example of the dynamics present in many churches. The problem is as old as the Scriptures themselves, where Paul defends his own presentation to the Corinthian church.

> When I came to you, brothers, I did not come with eloquence or superior wisdom as I proclaimed to you the testimony about God. For I resolved to know nothing while I was with you except Jesus Christ and him crucified. I came to you in weakness and fear, and with much trembling. My message and my preaching were not with wise and persuasive words, but with a demonstration of the Spirit's power, so that your faith might not rest on men's wisdom, but on God's power (I Corinthians 2:1-5).

Many Christians evaluate pastors, evangelists, and teachers on their leadership, strength, persuasive words, and moving presentation. Perhaps we are frighteningly similar to the parents of Hamelin who invited the Pied Piper to relieve the suffering caused by the rats. We build programs, services, Bible studies, and conferences around personalities whose words will be irresistible, yet we wonder why our people foolishly follow various pied pipers to spiritual never-never lands.

Our attitudes toward a speaker can make us resemble a cult more than we like to think. Most cult leaders exude charisma, personality, and class. They are able to make a follower feel "the presence of God."

To complicate matters, Christian media— both print and broadcasting—often present only success stories of leaders with overwhelming drive and ability. We must remember that these media of communication have a catalyst in common: marketing.

Scripture was not written with Madison Avenue-type marketing in mind. It records the weaknesses and struggles of God's leaders.

In the sixties there was a popular television program about a character who was half-man, half-machine called "The Six Million Dollar Man." After watching the show with my ten-year-old daughter, we discussed what a "bionic man" was. As we were talking I turned the TV dial to a channel broadcasting an electronic parachurch program. We both listened as the pastor told of his miraculous delivery from a tragic accident. Other passengers lay suffering with pain, even dying. But he just raised his hands, praised God, and climbed out without receiving even a scratch—because of his faith. My daughter exclaimed, "Wow! They even have bionic pastors."

"Yes," I replied, "but remember, bionic people are half machine."

Jesus bled when He was hurt. He calls us to suffer for and with our fellow Christians. He also rose with scars to remind us that our suffering is understood.

The mud and mortar of the foundations of all the groups mentioned in the first chapter of this book were made of the perfect church (usually independent) and a powerful leader who, because there was no system of checks and balances, was finally placed in a position beyond confrontation. Most cults allow one or more leaders to confront the laity and call them to accountability, but never the reverse. Ultimately, this dynamic results in followers giving over to leaders the complete control of their minds and lives. In many cases leaders are granted more authority over personal matters than Scripture allows.

In an interview with the *Wittenburg Door,* Ronald Enroth, sociologist at Westmont College, stated:

> The students I see in religious colleges have come through a long string of leaders. I am not saying these leaders have been had, but the kids have come to expect leaders to provide packaged Christian answers for them. So they come to a religious college expecting to write down everything the "Christian" professor says *without question*. I do not think we have encouraged Christian young people to think for themselves and we need to teach young people to think critically. We need to encourage young people to make decisions on their own. We need to help the young person develop a personal autonomy [italics added].[2]

Enroth has hit the nail squarely on the head. All of us are guilty of looking to the right seminar, teacher, pastor, shepherd, or workshop for instant answers to the complex questions of life.

At a national pastors' conference I attended

not long ago, all the participants concurred that more and more people were asking the pastors to make crucial decisions for them. This kind of student usually comes from a congregation that has been built around a powerful pastor or leader. This phenomenon in the church is nothing new. Groups have often centered around a spiritual authority who has furthered his or her personal goals. Leaders of such groups often are impelled by genuine beliefs in their ideas, insights, discoveries, and spirituality as being the solutions and answers to the complex problems and ills of society. If the group believes that members can become sinless, the leader, of necessity, must be blind to the fault of his or her own impure motives in dominating and wielding power over others, otherwise their whole foundation falls. If the leader isn't sinless, what is the hope for the laity? This blindness, subtle manipulation, and control is not limited to extreme cults like the People's Temple and the group in Waco, Texas. Blind abuse of power is also evident in many Christian circles.

Enroth offers a clue as to how and why this can be.

The popularity of evangelical gurus, new-age cults, and superpastors says a number of things about our society as well as rank-and-file evangelicalism. First, there are many people in our rapidly changing and often confusing world who have real dependency needs. They are attracted to authoritarian movements, Christian or otherwise, because these movements offer black and white, clear-cut answers (or systematized approaches) to life's problems. Moreover, the leaders of such organizations convey a sense of solidity, a feeling of being on top of problems, of being in control of the situation. In a word, these groups offer security. For people who have lacked positive structure in their lives, who have difficulty making decisions or resolving conflicts or who are just plain uncertain about the future, these movements, churches/ programs are a haven.[3]

If leaders teach submission, obedience, and a strong chain of command without understanding or admitting their own motives, they may become pied pipers leading needy people to a never-never land.

I'm Not Responsible!

Recently I spoke to a woman in deep emotional and spiritual distress. Her problem? She could no longer function, make decisions, pray, and reach out to others because her spiritual shepherd, who for three years had told her what she could and could not do, had moved out of town. She was no cult member; she was active in a prominent church in the Boston area.

My first response to her was: "I understand the Bible to say 'The LORD is my shepherd.' Perhaps you have allowed your mortal pastor to take Christ's place."

I personally agree with those who see the benefits of counseling. But I see a danger in asking a counselor, pastor, or friend to be responsible for making personal decisions. This is another old problem—as old as the story of Adam and Eve, who blamed each other for their predicament.

On Judgment Day we will be called to give an account of our own lives. I will have to take responsibility for my own choices and decisions. The same will be true for you. We will not be able to weasel out by saying,

"Lord, don't judge me. Judge my shepherd."

Many shepherds and disciples provide not only counsel, but control. They often use God's name in vain by saying, "I have a direct word from the Lord concerning you." Again notice what Enroth has to say on this matter:

> When a "delegated authority" provides counsel to those under him, he speaks with God's authority. As Derek Prince, a leader in the discipleship movement, puts it: "Whenever his (God's) delegated authority touches our lives, he requires us to acknowledge and submit to it, just as we would to him in person." Or, as John Robert Stevens of "The Walk" describes it, "If the authority over you is submissive to God, then you are to be submissive to him with your very life."[4]

Does this sound similar to Jonestown? To Waco?

When Paul was told by believers that he should not go to Jerusalem, he took that as information, not as an imperative or command. He still went to Jerusalem.

Cult members and Evangelicals often have

difficulty admitting that their own leaders are broken people, vulnerable to human frailty and sin. I have pastored in several churches; some were Evangelical, but two were liberal on a journey toward a deeper biblical commitment. I saw one major cultural difference between the Evangelicals and the liberals. As a rule, the liberals faced issues openly, admitted their wrongs, and sought forgiveness, whereas many Evangelicals tended to justify or spiritualize their behavior or blame the church authorities and structures for the group's shortcomings and sins. Our inability to deal with our weaknesses and sins as a movement and in our leaders makes us extremely vulnerable to exploitation of leadership similar to that of cults and totalitarian political groups.

Many people were disturbed by the tragic events of Jonestown and Waco. Questions were asked: How could this happen in a religious community or church? What circumstances allowed a person, in the name of religion, to use, exploit, and so blatantly control others? One theme recurred throughout the stories of Jim Jones and David Koresh: power without checks and balances. It is so easy to write Jones off as unorthodox, pathological (perhaps insane), or just demonically cruel. But are they really so different from many of us? We may forget that we are equally capable of building up churches and concepts of spirituality that exploit others, that pit friends against friends, and, on a smaller scale, strive to build subtle power kingdoms that include no checks and balances.

Power!

God entrusts all of us with some form of power. The misuse of that power is probably the most overlooked and common sin in the Evangelical church today.

In his book *The Violence Within,* Paul Tournier addresses this "will to power" that is so evident in religious groups. He says, "They look upon us as experts, God's mouthpieces, the interpreters of his will.... We find ourselves thinking that when they follow our advice they are obeying God, and that when they resist us they are really resisting God."[5]

We all have clay feet. We are all vulnerable to being exploited or exploiting. We all need proper checks and balances to keep leadership in a proper perspective. Paul began by placing the total counsel of God over his life. He said, "I have not hesitated to proclaim to you the whole will of God" (Acts 20:27). Many

churches and cults have been built around one
aspect of Scripture that was deemed supremely
important by the founder. Some cults overly
emphasize the inerrancy of Scripture, others
teach mainly the Second Coming, some ham-
mer away at the importance of healing, and
most cults emphasize evangelism and missionary work.

Ben Patterson, a Presbyterian pastor, stated
this most clearly in an article in the *Wittenburg
Door.*

> Cultic thinking subscribes to the
> domino theory of Christian doc-
> trine. Topple one and everything
> else collapses. This introduces yet
> another kind of error. If every doc-
> trine is as weighty as every other
> doctrine, i.e., if a doctrine of...
> angels is of the same weight as a
> doctrine of the deity of Christ, then
> nothing is weighty. It is like the
> aphorism, if everyone is the boss
> then no one is boss....
>
> If every doctrine is equally
> important, then any doctrine has a
> claim to be the center around which
> a group organizes itself. And what is

a cult, but something that has organized itself around a false center?[6]

The Word of God, the Bible as a whole, is the proper guide for our discerning whether or not a teacher is "kosher." When a mesmerized audience or congregation are not thinking in a critical manner about what a pastor with great charisma is saying, they can accept without question statements that can not even be verified by the Bible as absolute truth.

I recently heard a well-known Evangelical pastor make the following statement on a Christian radio station: "God has raised up America for a witness to the world."

Certainly we hope this is true, but the Bible never specifically spells out the role of the United States. When we unquestioningly accept statements such as these as being absolute, we unknowingly take baby steps away from the biblical authority on which we should firmly stand. We make the words of pastors, evangelists, or teachers equal to or greater than the words of Scripture.

We need to keep our teaching as broadly based as Paul, being careful to encompass the full counsel of God. If a church's message is centered around the pastor's special concern for "body life," balancing adjustments need to be made so that worship is taught and practiced. If relational theology is a church's focus, the base should be expanded to include the teaching of historic theology. This helps keep both church members and special-emphasis leaders from exploiting others.

All Authorities Are Vulnerable

What does Scripture say about leadership? One thing is quite clear: The leaders of God needed to be confronted. Moses stood under the law of the Ten Commandments. David was confronted by Nathan. Peter followed the Galatians to another gospel sometime after Pentecost and was called to account by Paul.

Steve Larson writes,

> Moses is not singled out in Scripture as one whose response of inferiority in the face of the Lord's mission of leadership leads to a grand unleashing of the Lord's power. A quick survey of the Bible reveals that recognition of weakness, and consequent dependence upon God's strength, looms as the significant factor in the potency of many biblical leaders:

Gideon:

"And the Lord turned to him and said, 'Go in this might of yours and deliver Israel from the hand of Midian, do not I send you?' And he said to him, 'Pray, Lord, how can I deliver Israel? Behold, my clan is the weakest in Manasseh, and I am the least in my family.' And the Lord said to him, 'But I will be with you, and you shall smite the Midianites as one man.'" (Judges 6:14-16)

Saul:

"When Samuel saw Saul, the Lord told him, 'Here is the man of whom I spoke to you! He it is who shall rule over my people.' . . . Saul answered, 'Am I not a Benjaminite, from the least of the tribes of Israel? And is not my family the humblest of all the families of the tribe of Benjamin? Why then have you spoken to me in this way?'" (I Samuel 9:17, 21)

David:

"And David said to Saul, 'Who am I, and who are my kinsfolk, my father's family in Israel, that I should be son-in-law to the king?'... And Saul's servants spoke those words in the ears of David. And David said, 'Does it seem to you a little thing to become the king's son-in-law, seeing that I am a poor man of no repute?'" (I Samuel 18:18, 23)

John the Baptist:
"He must increase, but I must decrease" (John 3:30)

Paul:
"And I was with you in weakness and in much fear and trembling; and my speech and my message were not in plausible words of wisdom, but in demonstration of the Spirit and of power, that your faith might not rest in the wisdom of men but in the power of God" (I Corinthians 2:3-5).

The leaders in Scripture were not only weak at the initial call from God, they were *continuously weak* (Larson's italics).[7]

The power of God given to these leaders

was poured into vessels that were permanently weak. These models in Scripture are the opposite of the superstars of cults and of some Christian groups. The antithesis of the misuse of power is gentleness, which is best seen and understood within the framework of strength. Gentle leaders, pastors, or teachers do not force their insights and wisdom on the unlearned, nor flaunt their gifts before those in need. They are patient. They take time for those who are slow to understand. They are compassionate with the weak, and they share with those in need. Being a gentle pastor, shepherd, leader, or teacher is never a sign of being weak, but of possessing power clothed in compassion.

The great mystery of the Incarnation was not the performance of Christ's spectacular miracles; it was His restraint of power over others. Being very God of very God in the form of man, He could at any moment have breathed His enemies off the face of the earth. His meekness is perhaps the greatest manifestation of God's gentleness. Christ possessed divine power over others, yet He refused to use it—even when challenged by Satan and the crowds to prove to them physically that He was the Son of God.

True Marks of Leadership

Quick answers that cut like swords and control like guns are not signs of a speaker's wisdom, but of arrogance, insecurity, and a refusal to face his or her weakness and sin. Because God's purpose is not to control but to encourage, not to tear down but to redeem, God's power is always coupled with gentleness, patience, and compassion.

Jesus Christ is to be our model and our only Shepherd. Jesus calls Himself the Good Shepherd (John 10:11). A good shepherd leads, rather than controls, the flock.

Satan tempted Christ to separate ends from means, to prove a victorious leadership by side-stepping the Cross and the pain of relationships, misunderstanding, and time. Christ responded, "For it is written: 'Worship the Lord your God, and serve him only'" (Matthew 4:10). Note that Jesus connects worship and service. Love for God and compassion for others are central in the life of Jesus and should be at the heart of healthy leaders and churches. Any Christian group that does not spark compassion and love for God will probably lose its direction. Any group that creates arrogant, belligerent people should immediately be suspect. Unbelievers

felt comfortable in God's presence and sought
Him out. Being committed to Christ means that
unbelievers feel comfortable in our presence.

Jesus is the true model of authority served.
In the New Testament, the Greek word *exousia*
("authority") does not imply any jurisdiction
over the details of others' lives. Rather, it
implies the authority of truth, wisdom, and
experience that can be evidenced in a leader
who is held up as a special example. Peter
encourages Christians to "be shepherds of
God's flock that is under your care,... not
lording it over those entrusted to you, but
being examples to the flock" (1 Peter 5:2-3).
In Acts 20:30 Paul warns that "even from your
own number men will arise and distort the
truth in order to draw away disciples after
them." Abuse of the discipleship concept
began in the first century.

Look at Yourself

Leaders who are most gentle, mature, and
wise usually are those who are harder on themselves than on their flocks and congregations.
Leaders who are not at war against their own
sinfulness and the temptation to control others
will soon seek to control and destructively project their own weaknesses onto others. If we

are in positions of power over others and we fail to place controls on ourselves, we subtly and unknowingly start to control others. Power that elevates a leader beyond contradiction or check to a bionic position will lead both the leader and the followers down a road marked by broken relationships, exploitation, and control. Power that tempers and checks itself and is wrapped in compassion is the pathway to gentleness, caring, and maturity. Jesus said, "I am the Good Shepherd. The good shepherd lays down his life for the sheep" (John 10:11). He is our model of service and leadership.

7

You Are God's Sheep, Not the Pastor's

A major problem in the church is that people resist being accountable to others. Often this is sparked by an attitude of independence. However, a more serious problem is that when a person makes a decision to be accountable, that willingness is taken advantage of or abused by church leadersa and people in positions of authority.

Ponder the following questions:

 — Have you ever had a Christian leader imply that you were either rebellious or disobedient to God because you didn't take their advice?
 — Have you ever had a Christian leader tell you that you had an evil spirit or a spirit

of rebellion simply because you asked
questions?
— Have you ever challenged a teacher or
leader and they saw this as an assault on
their authority?
— Have you ever felt that a leader (or leaders) was (were) lording it over you?
— Does it ever bother you when a Christian
group, community, or Bible study all
look, act, and talk like the leaders?

If any of these questions ignites a positive
response in you, you may be involved in an
aberrant or potentially destructive relationship,
group, or church. In this chapter I will examine the New Testament's practical guidelines
given to protect us from getting entangled in
relationships where deception and manipulation can be used to guide us both emotionally
and spiritually.

When I have helped people who have been
taken advantage of by authority figures, I have
noticed a common biblical justification for
the abuse. The biblical metaphor of a shepherd caring for the flock is often at the heart of
the matter.

The Good Shepherd

Jesus challenged Peter to follow him.

> "Simon, son of John, do you truly love me more than these?"
> "Yes, Lord," he said, "you know that I love you."
> Jesus said, "Feed my lambs."
> Again Jesus said, "Simon, son of John, do you truly love me?"
>
> He answered, "Yes, Lord, you know that I love you."
> Jesus said, "Take care of my sheep."
> The third time he said to him, "Simon, son of John, do you love me?"
> Peter was hurt because Jesus asked him the third time, "Do you love me?"
> He said, "Lord, you know all things: you know that I love you."
> Jesus said, "Feed my sheep."

Jesus did not say, "Feed *your* sheep," but "Feed *my* sheep." We are God's sheep, not any pastor's, elder's, or other leader's. This picture of sheep and shepherds is not the only metaphor given in the Bible. Some authoritarian churches and discipleship groups imply that sheep are too ignorant to receive direction from God and therefore need shepherds to tell them what to do. *The New Testament was written to all believers, not just leaders.* The picture of a shepherd and a flock is used twenty times in the Bible. However, sons or daughters is used over fifty times; saints, over sixty times; priests, conquerors, overcomers, believers, and a body, many times as pictures of the church. To overemphasize any one metaphor as the ideal at the exclusion of others will give a lopsided view of leadership. We need to keep our eyes on Christ and not on the human leader. The goal of all Christian training is to be conformed to the image of Jesus Christ and not the pastor, teacher, or another popular person in the church.

To overemphasize the characteristics of a shepherd and a flock, exclusive of other metaphors, can imply some alliances that are unhealthy and unscriptural. Paul voiced the words to first-century believers to not be anxious about bringing their anxieties to God in prayer. He emphasized going to God, not just a leader or shepherd (Philippians 4:4-6). Paul asked the Ephesians to pray for him. However, he did not ask them to make decisions for him. James said if anyone lacked wisdom, they were to go to God who gives it generously. He didn't say go only to the church leadership or even himself for wisdom (James 1:5). Jesus only is the head shepherd of the church.

Jesus is also pictured as the head of a body—the Church. Each hand moves independently of the other hand. Each finger and each foot moves independently of the other finger or foot. The head gives the instructions. One finger does not have to ask the other finger permission to move. The nerves and muscles in the arm move the finger but never the will of the arm. It is always from the head, who is Christ.

Problems Did Not Cause Despair

Difficulties surfaced between Peter and Paul before the whole community (Galatians 2:11-14), between Paul and Barnabas over John Mark (Acts 15:36-40), and between Paul and the Corinthians over many issues (2 Corinthians). These problems did not end their relationships, nor cause despair that the unity was not achieved instantly.

Leaders May Need to be Challenged

Peter was answerable to others. He carefully explained his position to eat with and baptize Gentiles. He did not assume that the position

of an Apostle was beyond question. He
explained his behavior and responded to their
inquiries. He did not see this challenge as an
assault on his post of leadership (Acts 11:1-4).

Paul expected and even encouraged the
Corinthians to examine, judge, and evaluate
his teaching to see if they were correct or not
(I Corinthians 10:15). When Peter, who was an
Apostle before Paul, moved from grace to legalism as the way of faith, Paul confronted and
challenged him. Paul did not say, "I cannot
question thosein authority over me" (Galatians
2:11-14). Peter was open and answered questions about his behavior, beliefs and interac-
tion with Cornelius. As a result, the Apostles
and Elders met to examine and conside the
issue a couple of times and there were many
questions and disagreements. They did not fall
into despair, lay guilt on themselves, bind the
devil, nor pray for more faith because they
were having disagreements or questions about
Peter's actions. Most importantly, they did not
say, "Peter is a spiritual authority over us so we
cannot question him" (Acts, chapters 11 & 15).

Elders were expected to be responsible to
counsel, encourage, and correct people on a
personal level. However, all believers are
encouraged to do exactly the same thing. Paul

encouraged believers to do exactly the same
thing (II Timothy 4:2; Galatians 6:1-5;
Colossians 3:16). We are to esteem those in
leadership and influence over us. However,
they are to be overseers by example, not
deception, nor manipulation.

No Church Leader or Structure Will Usher in Utopia

Paul and Barnabas refused to follow a legalistic dictum of unanimity when it violated their
individual convictions. As a result, they went
separate ways in ministry (Acts 15:36-39).
Problems will always exist in the church and
need to be faced and confronted. This
includes all leaders as well. The call to put on
compassion, kindness, humility, gentleness,
patience, and forgive each other grievances
assume that problems will be there, but so will
Jesus Christ to help us face them (Colossians
3:12-15). GOD IS THE ONLY PERSON
WHO NEVER HAS TO APOLOGIZE. IF
PETER COULD GO OFF BASE, AFTER
PENTECOST, SO CAN LEADERS TODAY—
including each of us and our churches.

The Early Church and Closed Meetings

A consistent mark of aberrant leaders of
groups is the mark of "one-upmanship"

expressed in the attitudes of the authority figures. The leaders, shepherds, authority figures
have special hidden truths not available to the
common folk in the church or community.
This attitude frequently leads to closed meetings for the "deeply spiritual" or "in-crowd."

When Jesus took his disciples out on special
retreats, often large crowds were allowed to go
along and observe, learn and listen. On one
occasion, five thousand people went with him.
Jesus taught them all the same things. The
"in-crowd" of the disciples did not have
greater truths belonging only to a select few at
these retreats.

Jesus did not force the disciples to submit to
him. He always left them with their personalities and attitudes. Do you ever feel forced to
submit to the leaders in your church or guilty
if you question them on issues? If so, you may
be headed for a journey to a hideous landscape
of control and manipulation under the guise of
spirituality.

Jesus went to the garden to pray and asked
the disciples to wait for him, but they fell
asleep. His shepherding program left them
with wills of their own. They chose to sleep.
He did not give up on them, force them to
accept His will in the matter, or lay guilt on

them later for not supporting the prayer ministry, prayer vigil, or concert of prayer (Matthew 26:37-46).

During Judas's betrayal, Jesus did not command Judas to submit and straighten up (Matthew 26:47-50). He allowed him to break rank and to rebel.

The disciples rebuked a man because he was not one of their shepherding group. Jesus rebuked them for this. He informed them that the man was of him even though he was not in their discipleship group. Jesus didn't permit them to identify themselves in opposition to another believer (Mark 9:38).

After the Crucifixion, the disciples were so disorganized and bewildered that they did not even recognize Jesus as the Christ. If Jesus had exercised a strong authority over them, they would have been forced to believe in the Resurrection.

The disciples gave Thomas the same freedom to worship with them even though he doubted. They did not pressure him to believe. They allowed the Lord the freedom to speak for Himself—and He did! They did not expel the doubter from their ranks. Thomas avoided superficial belief and refused to separate the Jesus of the disciples' experience from the

Jesus of space, time, and history. He had freedom to question, to doubt, and resolve his
issues. Thomas was not disloyal to the group
simply because he questioned their experience
and teaching. This could have been a public
relations disaster for the disciples. They were
not worried about keeping up an upbeat front
and veneer of spirituality (John 29:24-31). Do
people have that freedom in your fellowship
group, Bible study, or church?

Also, Paul makes sure that we understand
that unbelievers were present in the meetings
of the first-century church (I Corinthians
15:16). God called Paul directly. He didn't
use the apostles to speak for him and call Paul.

Ananias baptized Paul and he was called a
disciple, not a shepherd (Acts 29:10-18). There
is no evidence of shepherds (the Apostles)
indoctrinating Paul in closed meetings or
through cell group activities. There is no evidence that they told Paul he had to submit to
them. You will not find any evidence of "super
submission" programs in the New Testament.

Guidelines for Leaders

Peter saw the potential for leaders to take
advantage of people. At the close of his life,
he penned warnings and guidelines to leaders
in the first-century church.

To the elders among you, I appeal as a fellow elder, a witness of Christ's sufferings and one who also will share in the glory to be revealed. Be shepherds of God's flock that is under your care, serving as overseers—not because you must, but because you are willing, as God wants you to be; not greedy for money, but eager to serve; not lording it over those entrusted to you, but being examples to the flock. And when the Chief Shepherd appears, you will receive the crown of glory that will never fade away.

Young men, in the same way be submissive to those who are older. Clothe yourselves with humility toward one another, because,

> "God opposes the proud
> but gives grace to the humble."

Humble yourselves, therefore, under God's mighty hand, that he may lift you up in due time. Cast all your anxiety on him because he cares for you.

Be self-controlled and alert.

Your enemy the devil prowls around like a roaring lion looking for someone to devour. Resist him, standing firm in the faith, because you know that your brothers throughout the world are undergoing the same kind of sufferings.

And the God of all grace, who called you to his eternal glory in Christ, after you have suffered a little while, will himself restore you and make you strong, firm, and steadfast. To him be the power for ever and ever. Amen.

Peter states that we are not to be lording it over others, seeking status and power for ourselves. Lording it over others is worldliness. Leaders are to find their security and confidence in Christ not in a position of authority or power.

The New Testament assumes Elders and leaders will need to be confronted. They have a capacity to abuse their positions of authority. Paul told Timothy that there need to be several witnesses present when an accusation is made against an elder (I Timothy 5:19,20).

First, Peter says, Lording it over others is worldliness. Second, he says authority begins by identifying ourselves with the laypeople not in opposition to them. He labeled himself as a "fellows-elder," not as a senior elder. He identified himself as facing the same problems, suffering struggles, questions as they did. Like Jesus, he practiced incarnational servant leadership. These words were penned from a prison cell. You cannot force submission any more than you can force people to be moral or virtuous. You can, however, as a leader step into other people's world of daily living.

The imperative is clear, serve and not lord over others. Leadership is never lordship. God expects leaders to be open to others and aware of their own vulnerabilities. Peter saw these things as rooted in a greed for power or financial gain.

Leaders guard themselves by putting on humility. What comes to mind when you think of a humble person? One who is pious, devotional, and perhaps marked with a serene smile? Humility simply means to refuse power because it is there. Jesus' example of humility is clear.

> Your attitude should be the same as
> that of Christ Jesus:
>
> Who, being in the very nature of

God, did not consider equality with God something to be grasped,

but made himself nothing, taking the very nature of a servant, being made in the human likeness.

And being found in appearance as a man, he humbled himself and became obedient to death—even death on a cross.

Therefore God exalted him to the highest place and gave him the name that is above every name,

that at the name of Jesus every knee should bow, in heaven and on earth, and under the earth,

and every tongue confess that Jesus Christ is Lord, to the glory of God the Father (Philippians 2:5-11).

This passage lacks our culture's call for human rights. Today, "rights" are frequently driven by upward mobility. I have the right to have the same possessions and positions of those perceived higher than oneself. Jesus Christ set aside his power and stepped into our world. The greatest example of humility (the refusal to use power) was on the cross. Jesus could have destroyed everyone with one word.

Answers given by leaders in a spirit of arrogance to honest questioners can devastate and destroy people emotionally. Peter reminds leaders to humble themselves before God. Remember you are under the Hand of God, not Nero, not secularism, not the church. God takes words given in humility and, in time, exalts the teacher. Exalting follows a desire to serve. Leaders are encouraged to be strong in "the faith"—God's definition of grace, description of human nature, and explanation of the solution to the human problem. Often we confuse "our faith," "our experience" with "the faith." The Bible calls us to build others up in the knowledge of "the faith." The call is not to be strong in faith, but strong in "the faith."

Authority figures are then told to "be sober," "be alert," because Satan is there to deceive us about ourselves. Self-help programs may be good and insightful, but they can also be as deceptive as looking in the mirror. A gaze in a mirror is actually an illusion—a reversed reflection of ourselves. Everything looks the sames, but it is all inverted. As leaders we need to look into God's word to get God's picture of our vulnerabilities and potential hazards.

Where was Jesus tempted to abuse power

entrusted to him? In the temple. The hub of religious activity was the setting for Satan's second temptation to Jesus. The temple was the place where God's Word was manifest in the past. In this City of Peace sacrifices were offered, the temple was built. The holy city stood as a monument to God's work and promises in the past, present, and future. If our Lord was tempted to abuse power in the seat of religious activity, SO WILL WE WHO ARE ENTRUSTED with the responsibility. Satan will tempt us at religious activities and church services to manipulate, deceive, and control others under the shining varnish of spirituality. He tempts us to separate the ethics of our methods and the way we treat people from the final results. He tempts us to prove ourselves as authorities over others.

We all want to take shortcuts. There are quick and easy means of food preparation, tax preparation, learning, financial success, and the accumulation of facts. When we attempt to take shortcuts in leadership by abusing power, we will experience the death of all that God created to be meaningful in nurturing and growing relationships between pastors and parishioners, teachers and students.

Resist Deception and Manipulation in the Church

Effective manipulation, deception and mind control stems more from daily relations in the church rather than from exquisite mind-altering seminars, hypnosis, or crass indoctrination. Mind control and deception begin to happen when information is systematically hidden, withheld, or distorted, making unbiased decisions of discernment difficult. This happens in political groups, in advertising, in the media, in the classroom and church.

God has created us all to be in meaningful relationships; the inner desire to bond with others, can make us vulnerable to those who use rewards such as smiles, praise, or a gentle touch to subtly present their agenda of control, deception, and manipulation. Few believers, especially new converts, want to be seen as ignorant, uncultured, untalented, or unspiritual. The more concerned we are about being seen as such the more likely we are to take on the beliefs of those around us to avoid rejection by them or being seen as immature. We are all vulnerable of succumbing to unquestioned protocol which can lead us to abandon our own discerning judgments.

It is a fact of life that those "in authority"

define reality for the rest of us, whether that be in the political arena, the media, or in church. Perhaps this is why the New Testament calls us over and over again to be wise, discerning, and prayerful. A discerning eye is fundamental for one to check compelling social and religious pressures. When people behave simply as they are expected to do, it becomes hard for us to evaluate their actions critically or be the one who questions what is expected in the situation.

Many notable politicians, for example, supported pastor Jim Jones without questioning why he was always surrounded by guards, why People's Temple had locked doors and why newcomers were searched before being approved by the Welcoming Committee.

At a recent Christian Booksellers Convention, a well-known pastor appeared to sign his book and arrived with a cadre of bodyguards. Many at the convention thought it both amusing and novel. Few asked why a pastor would need bodyguards. Are we any different in our benightedness?

We must learn to observe discrepancies between the theories people advocate and their daily practice and behavior. Competent manipulators and those who succumb to deception will harbor their intentions surrounded by "normal" or perhaps "spiritual" appearances. It may be through a soft voice on the phone selling a product, or a person soliciting for a good cause.

Going passively along "on automatic" can be a major snare. We make assumptions in a situation. We fail to check out the reality of the situation and how it is impacting us.

Actively monitor social interactions. Practice thinking ahead of what will come next, checking discrepancies. Be aware of who is controlling whom in Bible studies, church meetings, and other social situations, to what end and what cost. Never accept vague generalities and inadequate explanations in response to your questions or challenges. Re-examine yourself when an answer is given to your questions and is actually confused, ambiguous, perhaps intentionally so, especially if someone suggests "you are just too unlearned to comprehend." It is good to seek outside information about a group, church, or Bible study before you join them.

Many of the most convincing appeals and deception are based on making others feel afraid, anxious, or guilty. No matter who the authority figure is, one should avoid getting pressured into unwanted confessions. Also, avoid making major decisions when you are under stress or confused, particularly in the presence of the person who has triggered the emotional reaction. Tell them you'll decide later.

One evening there was a knock at the door and the person there was soliciting funds for a group to protect the environment. First, I noticed the paper she had listed names of neighbors that showed how much they had given. Second, when I asked about the neighbors' confidentiality, the response was immediately that I certainly would be concerned about the environment. My question was sidestepped through sweet talk about the environment. Gnawing feelings of guilt were being used to provide a powerful impetus for soliciting a response in me. Third, I asked what percentage of the funds given went toward administration and how much was actually given to helping the environment. To my surprise, there was an outburst of rage and anger. I asked for more information so I could examine my reactions and then send a donation later. At that point the person walked away. Later, I asked the neighbors whose names were on the list if they had given. They all said the list was two years old. None had given for two years.

Also, I called the Boston Better Business Bureau and found out that the organization was basically a lobbying association and those going door-to-door were being paid a percentage of the money they raised.

Deception can come under the guise of good and just causes—even Christian causes. We need to be wary of those who overemphasize how free you are to choose among the options they present. Choosing Tums over Maalox is not the same as deciding whether you have stomach problems.

Question commitments if they are no longer appropriate for you. Sometimes a change of church activities can give one a breath of fresh air, new life, and a fresh beginning. Build some relationships with those outside your community who will keep you accountable, not buy your group religious jargon, and challenge any false sense of security thay you may be developing. When we are isolated from outside relationships and information, it is possible for us to fail to make unbiased decisions.

When we worship God and seek to be controlled by God's will, we can learn to use our power as an opportunity for service to others. The great mystery of the ministry of Jesus was that His was not a call to misuse or worship power, but to serve God in powerlessness.

When tempted to abuse power, Jesus responded by saying, "You must worship the Lord your God and serve Him alone." These words are reminders that only undivided attention to God Almighty can stem our own desire for expediency, manipulation, deception, and power. Without this foundation, we will be tempted to be self-seeking, manipulative, and deceive ourselves into believing that these opportunities for power over others are all for the sake of ministry. When we dress up our power in clichés and robes of false humility, we delude ourselves into believing we are serving while actually we are protecting our own interest.

Even in the church, Satan may call us to pit ourselves against others with idealistic affirmations that we are being "faithful to God's truth." While willfully blind to our own craftiness and hankering for power, we vainly use God's name to justify personal actions of manipulation or control. The temptation is there because both the society and the church are competitive and consumer-focused.

Jesus faced the very temptations that we face daily. He stood against sensationalism, deception, and control. That is the ultimate extreme of God's love for humankind. Christ identified with our struggles, and that path led to the final paradox of death on a cross between two thieves. Our world worships power, position, and upward mobility and sees these as the ultimate marks of success. Our generation has a hard time comprehending a kind of success that is based on a refusal to use others or to be used by others. Yet that is what God calls us to be and do when in posts of leadership and authority.

8

But Mormons Don't Drink or Smoke

Terry was an active leader in the youth group of the first church I served in California. He had become a Christian the previous year and gave a glowing testimony.

Then, astonishingly, Terry became a Mormon; he joined the Church of Jesus Christ of Latter-day Saints. My education and inexperience had left me ill-prepared to meet a crisis like Terry's. I still remember my confusion and dumfounded reaction to his defense: "But Mormons don't drink or smoke."

As with many American Christians, Terry's conversion to Christianity included adoption of specific cultural taboos important to American Evangelicals. These taboos, along with the popular emphasis on personal happiness and group support, confused Terry in his journey toward spiritual maturity. Terry isn't alone in his misguided journey.

Why do many Christians confuse the issues? It could be because we fail to give adequate instruction about the reasons for the convictions. We succeed in giving only inadequate teaching about spirituality. To Terry, those in the Mormon Church showed more consistency in keeping these convictions, deeper group commitment, and more genuine happiness and sincerity. Terry logically concluded, "They must be more Christian."

American Christians tend to yoke their definitions of spirituality with certain cultural convictions. For many, these "don'ts," ignored or barely mentioned in Scripture, become more important than moral issues and commandments clearly presented in God's Word. An overemphasis on taboos has misled some believers to feel more guilty about sipping a glass of wine than about sleeping with a boyfriend or girlfriend.

A young student from a well-known Boston Evangelical church sat in my office and tried to persuade me that the affair she was having with a married man was "directed of the Lord."

After all, through their love for each other he had accepted Jesus Christ as his personal savior. Something about our conversation seemed especially absurd, since just six months earlier she had told me of her disgust for Christians who attend theaters and dances.

This kind of lost perspective has made many Christians vulnerable to cults, because most cults hold to "Evangelical" convictions and offer familiar—but more rigid or intense—control and group commitment. In the documentary movie *Deceived,* Mel White interviewed former People's Temple members who told how the entire congregation was disciplined because one of their members had drunk a glass of wine. This striking similarity of values plays a major part in shifting one's loyalty to a cult. It is a major area of vulnerability for individuals and the church.

Our young people are not the only ones guilty of setting cultural convictions ahead of moral issues. An Evangelical author appeared on a popular Christian television program. At the time of the filming this man was separated from his wife and living in adultery (a fact known to many for several years, but overlooked because of the success of his ministry). The most bizarre part of the whole event was the discussion following the interview. The master of ceremonies on the program was having special prayer, asking God to deliver smokers from their habit. The Bible does command that we take proper care of our bodies, and concern for such is to be commended. But focusing on cigarette smoking without squarely facing biblical "thou shalt nots" is to misconstrue the Word of God.

Some years ago I attended a youth seminar where questions were asked about the importance of some of these Evangelical taboos. The seminar director commented that the closer one walks to Christ, the more one will accept these cultural taboos. How tragic that several years later, in the national news media, this same organization had to acknowledge that some of their staff members, over a period of years, had been involved in sexual sin and a misuse of funds that led to the organization's ruin. Did the emphasis on cultural issues blind them to other sins? This is a very painful issue for many of us to face, but it must be addressed. We cannot overlook this confusion between cultural convictions and biblical absolutes, but neither should we irresponsibly overreact and overthrow all taboos.

What has led to this confusion? Is it only a

problem of the twentieth century? Not really. Again we are discussing a problem as old as the Bible itself, and it centers around a misunderstanding of the nature of the Law.

Law and Grace

In both the Old and New Testaments, the Law points out our sin and disarms us by revealing our need for grace and absolutes to guide our lives. Christ expressly states He did not come to destroy the Law, but to complete it (Matthew 5:17).

In Romans, Paul states that we are not under law: "For sin shall not be your master, because you are not under law, but under grace" (6:14). At first glance this looks confusing. But note that the word law is not preceded by the article the. Whenever such an article is missing, the noun law speaks of a principle. Paul is saying that God accepts us, not because we do the right thing, but by and because of grace. However, He is not abolishing the absolutes of the Law itself. It is essential here to understand grace. Grace enables us to deal with our sin and live in obedience to God's absolutes. When we view law (getting God's acceptance by doing the right thing) instead of grace as the principle or means of acceptance, we place ourselves under the pressures of fear and rejection. At this point believers tend to set rules for themselves and in turn de-emphasize God's Law. These new selected restrictions, cultural taboos, and cultural convictions or rules become the new signs of spirituality. Over a period of time these can easily be given more importance than God's Word itself, and ultimately they can lead to legalism. Legalism always destroys the unity of the body of Christ that is given by God's grace. It always pits believers against each other. Spiritual hierarchies develop, and Christians are measured and accepted, not by commitment to God's grace and absolutes, but by how well they adhere to selected restrictions.

With the advancement of communications technology and the ease of travel, we have become more aware of how these voluntary restrictions vary from culture to culture. Consciences in one country or area are trained to feel guilty over things that are not at all condemned in other cultures. I am continually amazed by the many Evangelical institutions and churches that require members to sign pledges saying they will not indulge in such-and-such an activity, when that activity is not condemned in the Bible.

How unfortunate that they view Scripture so lowly! Perhaps such a pledge should list lust, greed, bitterness, gossip, fornication, adultery, hate, and other sins of the mind and flesh. After all, what really is worth enumerating or pointing out? Might our children eventually throw out the baby with the bathwater—throw out the biblical absolutes—thinking they are no more important than the culturally formed convictions? Or might they join a cult that encourages the pledging to which they have grown accustomed?

Restrictions vs. Legalism

This might sound contradictory, but I feel we need to place more restrictions on our lives. On every side our society bombards us with temptations to sin in thought and deed. Because we live in a relativistic society where biblical absolutes are ignored, we need to place voluntary restrictions on our lives without becoming legalistic.

When does one become legalistic? This serious question should not and cannot be avoided. Legalism was not invented by the Pharisees. It began in the opening chapters of Genesis, when Eve added her own restrictions to God's firm commands.

> "But you must not eat from the tree of the knowledge of good and evil, for when you eat of it you will surely die" (2:17).

> The woman said to the serpent, "We may eat fruit from the trees in the garden, but God did say, 'You must not eat fruit from the tree that is in the middle of the garden, and you must not touch it, or you will die'" (3:2-3).

In Genesis 2, God commanded only that Adam and Eve not eat any of the fruit. Note that by Genesis 3, Eve had decided she couldn't even touch the tree. But God had given no such prohibition; she had added to God's Word and made her own restrictions equal to His.

Voluntary restrictions on our lives are certainly important and often necessary. But whenever Christians or cult members make the same mistake as Eve, trouble starts brewing.

Admittedly, voluntary restrictions are usually the fruit of a sincere desire to do right and to protect oneself. There is nothing wrong with this. When we protect each other from temptation, we also encourage each other.

Restrictions become stumbling blocks when they are elevated to a position of equality with the Bible, when they are transferred from ourselves to others, and when they are prefaced with a verbal or strongly implied "God says."

When we let these restrictions become the basis for church membership, signs of spirituality, acceptance or rejection by a fellowship or community, we start controlling the lives of others. We start creating unhealthy dependence on our word, rather than on God's Word and judgments. In so doing, we devalue God's Word and we confuse future generations. We may have logical reasons why such-and-such a conviction makes sense, but when the restriction is preached without the rationale and without room for personal conscience, Christians start feeling guilty about breaking taboos and not about breaking God's absolute commandments. When we reach this point, we are strikingly similar to the cults.

What Is The Pattern?

The journey to heresy begins with a misunderstanding of God's grace and a lack of trust in His grace that enables us to keep His commandments. When we, rather than God, are responsible for keeping us in God's hands, we are constantly filled with fear. We are always afraid we will commit some minor infraction that will cause our damnation. Because we want to guarantee our purity, we place voluntary restrictions on ourselves and then on others, ultimately confusing them with God's Word. Finally we set them equal to God's Word. Eve, some Christian groups, and most cults share the problem of the Pharisees:

> So the Pharisees and teachers of the law asked Jesus, "Why don't your disciples live according to the tradition of the elders instead of eating their food with 'unclean' hands?" (Mark 7:5).

> "You have let go of the commands of God and are holding on to the traditions of men." And he [Jesus] said to them: "You have a fine way of setting aside the commands of God in order to observe your own traditions!" (7:8-9).

Were the disciples accused of breaking the law? No, not at all. They had merely failed to sign the pledge card saying they would wash their hands before each meal. They had broken the voluntary restrictions of the elders, who had elevated such "traditions" until they were signs of maturity, fellowship, and genuine spirituality.

Might this be the reason why Scripture says so little about the physical qualities of Jesus Christ? If Jesus had worn orange robes, we would no doubt have a holy color of dress. (I personally hate orange!)

In the sixties, I traveled with a mission team in Europe. We helped churches to establish "halfway houses" and coffee houses in order to reach members of the sixties' drug culture. I carefully observed the various Protestant subcultures: Some German Evangelicals drank beer, but criticized the French for drinking wine; the French drank wine while criticizing the Dutch Evangelicals for smoking; the Dutch criticized both the Germans and the French. On one occasion I spoke to a British Evangelical group who believed that during worship all women must cover their heads as a sign of submission. Ironically, that was the heyday of micro-mini skirts. While preaching, I wished I could stop and ask the women to take off their head coverings and place them over their laps. Their priorities seemed to be misnumbered. Certainly cultural taboos are needed in every age, but they are not to

become points of argument or the cause of
ridicule or strife. We must all remember that
the body of Christ is made up of many members, including people from many cultures.

Morally Absolute, Culturally Relative

Was the problem of taboos unique to Eve
and the Pharisees? No, Paul also had to face
this major issue as it related to church leaders
in various cultures. We must always remember that Scripture is inflexible morally but
flexible culturally. Morally the Bible is always
absolute; culturally it is relative. Fornication
was as wrong in Jerusalem as it was in
Corinth, but the eating of pork was a different
matter. The Jerusalem Christians abstained,
while the Corinthians freely ate it. Local convictions were determined by nationality—
whether or not one was Jewish or Gentile.

The best examples of Paul's cultural flexi-
bility are found in Acts and Galatians.

> He came ... to Lystra, where a dis-
> ciple named Timothy lived, whose
> mother was a Jewess and a believer,
> but whose father was a Greek. . . .
> Paul wanted to take him [Timothy]
> along on the journey, so he circum-

> cised him because of the Jews who
> lived in that area, for they all knew
> that his father was a Greek (Acts
> 16:1, 3).

> Yet not even Titus, who was with
> me, was compelled to be circum-
> cised, even though he was a Greek.
> This matter arose because some
> false brothers had infiltrated our
> ranks to spy on our freedom we
> have in Christ Jesus and to make us
> slaves. We did not give in to them
> for a moment, so that the truth of
> the gospel might remain (Galatians
> 2:3-5).

Paul understood the Jews and their cultural
restrictions. Since Timothy was part Jewish,
Timothy was circumcised. For the sake of
spreading the gospel Paul felt this outward
sign of Timothy's Jewish heritage was important. In the Acts account, Paul honors the cultural norms so the Jews would accept Timothy
as one of them.

But in Galatians Paul points out that Titus,
who is wholly Gentile, needn't be circumcised.
Was Paul being fickle? Why the difference?
Why did Paul here take a firm stand against

something he had insisted on in the case of
Timothy?

The answer is simple. The false teachers near
Galatia were following the example of Eve and
the Pharisees, who made laws of their personal
rules. Paul refused to give in to these teachers
who were preaching a false spirituality.

Central to all biblical instruction is our
responsibility to make right choices. We are
free to make any choice, but we are not called
to act on our every freedom. On occasion we
must place voluntary restrictions on ourselves.
Selected restrictions do not make us legalists.
We become legalistic only when we begin to
define mature Christianity on the basis of these
restrictions and when we use them as means
for accepting other Christians into our fellowship or excluding them from it.

Weaker Christians?

Liberty in Christ is not to be confused with
the liberation movements of our own culture.
Scriptural liberty is not an injunction to discover how many freedoms we have and to
flaunt them before others. Ours is a liberty to
be reconciled with God and others, even
with legalists. Ours is a freedom to be open
with God, a freedom to be obedient. Flaunting

freedoms has nothing to do with liberty or liberation; it is another form of enslavement, perhaps worse than that of the legalists.

A colleague tells of visiting a pastor who just had to show off his wine cellar. His newfound cultural freedom had become a newfound spiritual enslavement. In being proud of his freedom, he was abusing the liberty Christ gives His followers. Part of the freedom we have in Christ involves acting responsibly toward others who may be weaker than we.

We do have responsibility toward others, especially to the weaker Christian. The Christian life is a corporate life. As soon as we say the first word of the Lord's Prayer, we acknowledge that corporate reality. That one word our expresses our theology, responsibility, and relationship with others.

The concept of the stumbling block and the weaker Christian has been greatly misused and misunderstood and is often presented as meaning the opposite of Scripture's intent. We need to study the biblical definition of the "weaker Christian" and separate in our minds that phrase from the "older Christian" and his or her desire to control other people. Control is the heart of all cult groups, and it must not be overlooked as sin, even when it is disguised as concern for the weaker Christian.

Paul exhorts us to be concerned about weaker Christians; he does not exhort us to please legalists. Three Pauline passages address this issue and define the "weaker Christian." The first is in Romans.

> Accept him whose faith is weak, without passing judgment on disputable matters. One man's faith allows him to eat everything, but another man, whose faith is weak, eats only vegetables. The man who eats everything must not look down on him who does not, and the man who does not eat everything must not condemn the man who does, for God has accepted him.... One man considers one day more sacred than another; another man considers every day alike. Each one should be fully convinced in his own mind.... Therefore let us stop passing judgment on one another. Instead, make up your mind not to put any stumbling block or obstacle in your brother's way.... It is better not to eat meat or drink wine or

> to do anything else that will cause
> your brother to fall. So whatever
> you believe about these things keep
> between yourself and God.
> (Romans 14:1-3, 5, 13, 21-22).

According to this passage, the persons who place restrictions as signs of spirituality on their lives are the weaker Christians.

> We know that an idol is nothing.... But not everyone knows this. Some people are still so accustomed to idols that when they eat such food they think of it as having been sacrificed to an idol, and since their conscience is weak, it is defiled.... But food does not bring us near to God; we are no worse if we do not eat, and no better if we do. Be careful, however, that the exercise of your freedom does not become a stumbling block to the weak. For if anyone with a weak conscience sees you who have this knowledge.... This weak brother, for whom Christ died, is destroyed by your knowledge.... Therefore, if what I eat causes my brother to

> fall into sin, I will never eat meat
> again, so that I will not cause him
> to fall (I Corinthians 8:4, 7-11, 13).

Again, the weaker Christian is the one who
abstains. In this passage the cultural issue
involves the trappings of a past false religion
that equated spirituality with eating meat
offered to idols. Your eating meat may cause a
certain person to believe in a false religion,
may drive that weaker believer back to pagan
worship. Paul emphasizes concern for the
weaker Christian, who doesn't have the same
heightened knowledge and clearness of conscience as others who are free of extrabiblical
regulations. Stronger Christians place voluntary restrictions on themselves even when they
know these have nothing to do with spirituality
or church membership.

Later in I Corinthians Paul brings up the
matter again.

> If some unbeliever invites you to a
> meal and you want to go, eat what-
> ever is put before you without rais-
> ing questions of conscience. But if
> anyone says to you, "This has been
> offered in sacrifice," then do not eat
> it for conscience' sake—the other

man's conscience, I mean, not
yours. For why should my freedom
be judged by another's conscience?
(I Corinthians 10:27-30)

As you can see, the Word of God sheds a
bright light on how and why we regulate our
lives.

In the Book of Romans, Paul views as the
strong Christians those who know that meat
offered to idols has no special cultic power.
The gospel has freed them. Such a freed person could go to the temple market, buy the
best steak or the cheapest meat, and—even
though it had been offered to idols—eat it with
enjoyment. Why? Because of a seared conscience? No. Because of his or her knowledge and understanding of freedom in Christ.

What does Paul mean when he speaks of the
knowledge of the judgment of God? The freedom of walking in the Spirit? Law can't give
such freedom; only grace can assure us that
God is not offended when we eat such meat.
He does not condemn such cultural actions.

Blind in One Eye

We all have weak spots in our lives, usually
seen by others but not by ourselves. We are all

strong Christians in some matters and weak Christians in other areas of our lives. In these Pauline passages we are not invited to engage in activities blindly and compulsively just to prove our liberty.

The weak Christian is not the one who voluntarily abstains, but the abstainer who sees restrictions as the evidence of his or her (or someone else's) spirituality, the one who cannot exercise a freedom because of a misinformed conscience. The weak Christian is the one whose lips haven't touched cough syrup or perhaps vanilla extract (because of their alcoholic content) for fear they would call down the displeasure or wrath of God.

Paul recognizes that we all bring to the church some baggage accumulated in our younger years. Our past brokenness leaves a residue. Some of us may understand the differences between cultural, voluntary restrictions and biblical absolutes, yet we may not be able to enjoy and live in the freedoms God has granted. Our head knowledge may be ahead of our heart knowledge.

On the other hand, some of us who feel we have thrown off all constricting cultural taboos tend to go off the deep end and go out of our way to offend legalists (a sinful desire similar to the exploitation of cults). It is important to note that Scripture does not bind anyone to obey the legalist rules or give in to one's negative feelings about one's liberties.

If a person who has been a Christian for forty years believes it is a sin to go to a movie, you needn't be uptight. But then again, you should not deliberately flaunt your freedom or offend the person by telling them how great a recent film was at the local cinema.

These issues are not easy to address and not easy to resolve personally. Only with prayer, Bible study, honest self-evaluation, and soul-searching of our motives can we move toward freedom and wholeness in Christ.

Many of us would rather ask our pastor, church, or fellowship group to lay down life-long restrictions than to face the responsibility of making our own decisions. But convictions made by proxy never promote personal growth. They only produce immature Christians, create credibility gaps, and make us vulnerable to cults who function in a similar way.

A Greater Responsibility

As we strip away our legalism, discover our new liberties, and voluntarily select restrictions, we are forced to face the bare bones of the greater responsibility for which we will individually be accountable to God: "All men will know that you are my disciples if you love one another" (John 13:35).

We are to affirm the doctrine of creation and redemption to our families and to other believers—including legalists and older Christians who may seek to control us. At one time or another, all of us will have to make crucial ethical decisions. The group, pastor, cult leader, or fellowship group may not be there to say, "Thus saith the Lord." We must be ready to rest in the knowledge of God's Word, which will enable us to choose correctly, and then act on our choices.

> We proclaim him [Christ], admonishing and teaching everyone with all wisdom, so that we may present everyone perfect in Christ (Colossians 1:28).

9

The Problem of Pain

Every human has needs and desires they long to have filled and met. They want love, some sense of order, a purpose for and definition of life, some security. Some of these needs can only be met by God, but others can and should be filled by fellow humans and institutions.

Many cults, like many Christian groups, meet these personal needs. When answers— no matter whose they are—are dressed up in Bible verses, many of us turn off our discerning and critically thinking minds. We can be lured and deceived. Many false teachers "stand" on the Bible and claim to have a high view of Scripture, but they pick and choose their pet passages.

James W. Sire points out in his book

Scripture Twisting that the Bible is used by many modern cults, Hindus, and Buddhists. It is the final authority for Christian Scientists and Jehovah's Witnesses. It is quoted by Sun Myung Moon in his book *The Divine Principle.* It is read by Mormons.[1]

Many Christian churches are built around one aspect of Scripture. Such groups are in danger of treating the Bible as the cults do. This problem can result in leaving the church members susceptible to a group that emphasizes the same issue, even with the same biblical arguments. For example, a church that has been established with single-minded emphasis on biblical prophecy may make its members game for cults that center on similar prophetic Scriptures. Or the opposite may happen: Overemphasis on experience may make a person revel in a search for a doctrinal foundation. In that search the believer may be attracted to a cult that seems to be stabilized on a doctrinal structure. Or a church that emphasizes doctrine at the exclusion of warmth and devotion may drive a person under great personal stress into a cult that sincerely seeks to meet and minister to human needs.

My experience reveals that people involved in cults or attracted to groups with cultic leanings have been handicapped by an imbalance in past Christian experience and teaching. Perhaps the most evident is the difficulty many Christians have in facing suffering and affliction. We have been extremely guilty of taking sections of Scripture and using them to reinforce only one half of the biblical answer to the problem.

Charismatic and Holiness groups emphasize healing. In his book *The Disease of the Health and Wealth Gospels,* Gordon Fee says that certain elements of the neocharismatic movement who claim that no sickness is within God's will are in closer agreement with the teachings of Christian Science than with the whole of Scripture.[2]

On the other hand, Reformed and dispensational groups tend to emphasize the cathartic benefits of pain. They pride themselves in a kind of naturalism and fatalism that sees God working through circumstances as they are rather than His working to change circumstances.

If You're Not Healed, It's Your Own Fault

I am indebted to the Charismatic movement, because Charismatic Christians sparked my faith in Jesus Christ. Their faithful desire to teach the Scripture, their many answered prayers, their exemplary lives, the quality of their relationships—all made an early impact on my life and convinced me of the reality of the person and work of Jesus Christ. However, over the years I noticed a pattern that continued to bother me, a pattern that made many of their members open to guilt, despair, loss of faith, even to false teachings of cults.

The problem was this: If God healed a person, the evangelist or minister who prayed for the deliverance was acclaimed for having great faith; if God chose not to heal, the person who was being prayed for was accused of lacking faith. Those who weren't healed went away confused, discouraged, and feeling guilty. This discouragement and hurt was a direct result of teaching based on half of what Scripture has to say on the subject. God does answer prayer and He does heal. But His not healing does not mean that He hasn't answered the prayer.

We live in a generation that has been stripped of the real. We have been handed many synthetic substitutes for natural flowers, food, and cloth. Many prefer artificial flower arrangements over the real thing, for although plastic blossoms have little fragrance, they

never wither and die. Our food doesn't quickly spoil, and our synthetic clothes are never
eaten by moths.

How easy it is for us to transfer our expectations for the unreal to our thinking on spiritual
matters: No more trouble! Daily manna from
heaven. Dollar bills falling from the sky. No
suffering. No problems. This view of the
Christian life is lopsided.

On the other hand, some Evangelicals teach
that the Christian life is similar to life portrayed in Sartre's *No Exit*: Always the "heav-
ies," doom, gloom, God working mainly
through our trials and tribulations.

I am now an ordained minister in the
Reformed arm of the church. Here I see a lot
of this opposite, "hard times" Christianity that
claims God works—that is, prefers to work—
through our afflictions.

God certainly does work through our crises.
But when we view only one side of Scripture,
we are as guilty as those who say, "God must
heal." This position can also lead to despair
and fatalism. It can send Christians looking
for the green pastures on the other side in
hopes that they will find refreshment from
their suffering.

How does one stay firmly planted between

these two extremes? How does one live to God's glory in an age of anxiety? On what framework can we cultivate the art of living despite the fractured effects of the Fall? How can we be balanced, biblical believers?

The Sources of Affliction

The Bible offers several reasons why we experience difficulties, afflictions, and suffering. First, we live in a world that has been devastated by the Fall. The irrational and unjust muck of sin is passed on sociologically, genetically, and psychologically. The residue causes disorder, unfairness, unreasonableness, and injustice in every realm of reality. Children are born blind, disabled, and malformed. Disease haunts everyone, for we all carry some physical weaknesses; some of us are prone to diabetes, others to psychological disorders, others to cancer. Still others struggle with tendencies toward sexual deviations. Christians and non-Christians alike are influenced by their physiological, psychological, and sociological surroundings and beginnings. At one time or another everyone gets a cold and has a headache. Everyone bleeds when cut. All people, Christian and non-Christian, die physically. Since the Fall, all of life has been tainted by a persistent element of injustice.

Second, the Bible pictures life as influenced by unseen spiritual forces. Satan is a spiritual reality who acts in every age, plays on human minds, disturbs individuals, and influences nature, families, and world leaders. Satan's purpose is to sabotage God's redemptive work in history by infiltrating the world with sin, suffering, alienation, and confusion.

I was fascinated by a Chinese play I saw once in San Francisco. The stage had two levels. On the upper stage, evil and good spirits battled with each other. The actors on the lower stage could not see the war waging above them, but their actions and scripts were obviously influenced by the supernatural forces. What a fitting reflection of reality as presented in the Bible, where the battles of the unseen world are pictured as influencing every one of us.

Third, we have problems because our actions entail consequences. The mystical Eastern parables that tell of a person entering a body of water that doesn't ripple have no relation to reality. Our choices for good or ill do and will influence our future and the future of others. The destructive and chaotic choices of Hitler influenced the lives of many people.

The irresponsible drunk or drugged person who drives, hits another car, and cripples someone for life has influenced history for ill. The great spiritual and cultural reforms sparked by people such as Wilberforce, Luther, Martin Luther King, Jr., Wesley, and Calvin have changed the course of history for good.

We can bring unnecessary suffering to others. Young mothers who take drugs while pregnant and give birth to children with defects influence their family's history. Such ripples in the sea of life are real and very painful. God has created each one of us with such overwhelming significance that our actions cause real ripples that affect children, families, marriages, nations—every aspect of life for generations to come.

Last, God brings difficulties into our lives to help develop us, to strengthen us, to spark our growth, and to cultivate our maturity. The psalmist realized this when he said, "It was good for me to be afflicted so that I might learn your decrees" (119:71).

Do you see the complexity of the problem of suffering? How utterly impossible for us to know which issue or issues are the reason for our afflictions. Many causes may be at work at the same time. Scripture does not call us to sort out the "why" of someone's pain, but summons us to "weep with those who weep and rejoice with those who rejoice" (Romans 12:15, RSV).

Does God answer prayer? Of course He does. But not always on our terms or according to our definition. Like the picture drawn in the Chinese theater, the world is larger than one field of vision. Most of the time we are unable to sort through the causes of our situation. This is why we need to study God's Word, pray, and seek counsel from other Christians.

Jesus said, "In this world you will have trouble" (John 16:33). How easy it is for us to reflect the thinking of our society and expect all things to be resolved. Utopian expectations are the core of Nazism, Marxism, and all such "isms" that lead to dehumanization under the pretext of bringing happiness for all. Utopian expectations were the core of Jim Jones's Jonestown community and Stalin's purging of Russia.

Romans 8:28 says, "All things work together for good" (KJV). Note that Paul doesn't say that all things are good. We are not called to label everything that happens "good." Paul states a few verses later that nothing in this life can separate us from God's love found in

Christ Jesus—neither crisis, present history, future events, unseen forces, life, nor death. For the believer, life, spiritual forces, and death are part of a larger, good plan. Paul does not say that God's love takes away difficulties, but rather that it is with us when we are forced to rub against these raw edges of reality.

Puzzled Saints

Life has always been a complex puzzle. Even for God's leaders, solutions have never come easily. For their spiritual survival, believers have had to study, pray, exhibit compassion, and evaluate their own actions and motives.

The mysteries of life, the "whys," have always confounded great leaders of God. In the Old Testament, Habakkuk sets forth a complaint against God: "Your eyes are too pure to look on evil; you cannot tolerate wrong.... Why are you silent while the wicked swallow up those more righteous than themselves?" (1:13). Habakkuk doesn't understand why God's people go through difficulties.

If becoming a believer meant only receiving the promise of earthly goodies, wouldn't the whole world believe? Such misrepresentation of the gospel is more than unbiblical; it is naive. To claim such is similar to someone saying that sin is not fun. If sin weren't so pleasurable, why would anyone be sinning? Why would resisting temptation be so difficult?

Jeremiah—God's chosen prophet, leader of God's people, and spiritual model—found his mind grappling with these same puzzling questions: "You are always righteous, O Lord, when I bring a case before you. Yet I would speak with you about your justice: Why does the way of the wicked prosper? Why do all the faithless live at ease?" (12:1).

Do you ever ask why the wicked prosper? Jeremiah saw the gospel of "health and wealth and prosperity" as being tied to wicked and scheming people. In essence he was saying, "God, I am having difficulty with Your judgments. I just do not understand." How easy to disregard these questions and statements. But they are a part of God's Word—revelation given for our understanding. God did not condemn Jeremiah or Habakkuk for asking these probing questions, nor did He call into question their faith.

Answers Without Compassion

During a Bible study on the Book of Job, I heard a teacher comment, "The friends of Job misunderstood the causes of his affliction and laid guilt trips on him. We need to see what was going on from the divine perspective— that unseen forces were influencing the seen world. Job should have been able to see his situation in this light."

Although the theology was right, this teacher lacked a deep sensitivity to Job's confusion, difficulties, and hurts. Job didn't have the story of his life down on paper to read. Job didn't understand the "why" of all that was happening. In similar manner we do not always know which forces are at work and why. The important question is, How can God be glorified in this event?

Job couldn't pick up the book named after him and evaluate his own situation as being "just a spiritual battle." No, Job had the same need for compassion, understanding, and spiritual support that we do. He did not need to hear presumptuous assumptions. Simplistic or one-sided spiritual answers did not help Job, and they don't give us much help.

Some cult members and some Christians fall into the trap of assuming that they know all the causes of a particular affliction. But in this life we cannot know for sure. In this life we only "know in part" (I Corinthians 13:12).

Assuming that we know the cause of a sorrow can be a way of avoiding our difficult responsibility to cry with those who are crying.

How often do we assume we know the cause of other people's difficulties? Can you imagine Job's accusers saying, "You haven't been walking in the spirit"? Or "How is your spiritual breathing?" Or "Obviously your children haven't followed the right chain of command."

What was God's attitude toward Job? God lays it out in the first verse of the first chapter of Job's story: "In the land of Uz there lived a man whose name was Job. This man was blameless and upright; he feared God and shunned evil."

One friend of Job assumed the "obvious": If God were justly taking Job to task, Job would be suffering even more. God was obviously purging him, and even so, God had obviously overlooked some of his sins (see 11:1-6).

It seems another friend, agreeing with the first, had been schooled in basic confrontation counseling techniques and therapy. His "session" was similar to many in cults and questionable Christian groups, where someone's guilt is assumed. Job's friend said, "Your sin prompts your mouth; you adopt the tongue of the crafty. Your own mouth condemns you, not mine;

your own lips testify against you" (15:5-6).

To paraphrase, he was urging Job to admit his sin: "You are an evil man. Confess your sins; tell me and the group about them. You lack faith. If you had faith, you would possess health and wealth."

But remember, God thought otherwise: "In the land of Uz there lived a man whose name was Job. This man was blameless and upright; he feared God and shunned evil."

I Am Confused: I Do Not Understand

Job kept saying, "I do not understand or see the causes of these disasters." Job knew his accusers were wrong, yet they seemed blind to any conclusions other than their own presumptions. They could not hear Job's cries: "Look at me! Look at me! Can't you see the boils on my face? Here I am. My children are dead. Why? Why do other people's children live on?"

> Why do the wicked live on, grow-
> ing old and increasing in power?
> They see their children established
> around them, their offspring before
> their eyes. Their homes are safe
> and free from fear; the rod of God
> is not upon them (21:7-9).

Job had no answers. Yet, always wanting to see God glorified, he cast himself upon the sovereign God: "Though he slay me, yet will I hope in him" (13:15).

The Psalms are filled with similar questions. The psalmists understood the importance of acknowledging to God their confusion. They didn't stop there; they usually went on to proclaim God's sovereignty. The acknowledgment coupled with worship was the beginning of the healing of their perspective. The writer of Psalm 73 spills out his frustrations as he struggles with his loss of perspective, but ends in a doxology.

> When I tried to understand all this
> [the injustices of life], it was
> oppressive to me till I entered the
> sanctuary of God; then I under-
> stood their final destiny (Psalm
> 73:16-17).

Comforters who speak in platitudes and give simplistic answers avoid their responsibility to care, to minister, to be moved with compassion as modeled in Jesus Christ. The root of this avoidance is often related to our inability to deal with our own mortality. We are all terminal. Suffering people remind us that our own lives are fragile. The psalmists, Jeremiah, and Habakkuk knew this. They weren't afraid to be honest with God or ashamed of it. If God hasn't answered our prayer in the way we think He should have, God has still answered our prayer.

Our spiritual battle is no different from any other. It leaves behind wounded and disabled who will heal only if they are nurtured and cared for. When we fail to express compassion and concern to suffering people we come close to being guilty of shooting our wounded. Insensitivity, lack of compassion, and pat answers only deepen wounds. Such responses only make the wounded seek help elsewhere, possibly in some cult or other offbeat group that promises to meet these personal needs.

We all need to learn the art of listening. As God allowed Job and the prophets freely to express their anxieties, so should we. One of the best medicines for those in distress is the company of a good listener, someone who cares, prays, and does not immediately judge circumstances. Hasty judgments may cause us to overlook the boils on suffering faces; we are sure the sufferers are missing their quiet time, are failing to walk in the Spirit, have forgotten how to breath spiritually, or have hidden some secret sin. Let us not forget that those who suffer, live in poverty, face anxiety, and carry in their bodies afflictions may be like Job— blameless and upright.

Prayer and Faith

You may ask, "Doesn't James tell us to pray the prayer of faith for the sick?" Yes, but James 5:14 must be seen alongside the rest of Scripture. Jesus Christ encourages us to visit the sick. Speaking of the Last Judgment, the Book of Matthew reads:

> "Then the righteous will answer him, 'Lord, when did we see you hungry and feed you, or thirsty and give you something to drink? When did we see you a stranger and invite you in, or needing clothes and clothe you? When did we see you sick or in prison and go to visit you?'
>
> "The King will reply, 'I tell you the truth, whatever you did for one of the least of these brothers of mine, you did for me'" (Matthew 25:37-40).

Jesus Christ assumes that the sick and hungry will always be with us. He does not challenge us to legislate political change or to declare their lack of faith. He calls us to care for the needy as though they were Jesus Christ Himself.

Paul tells Timothy to take a little wine for his stomach's sake (I Timothy 5:23). He isn't implying that the water in his town is less than pure, but that Timothy suffered from some unhealed ailment—in fact, frequent illnesses.

Even after Pentecost, faith did not protect the disciples from suffering. The Book of Hebrews, for example, presents two sides of faith. Chapter 11 says,

> By faith Noah . . . built an ark (v. 7).
>
> By faith Abraham . . . was enabled to become a father (v. 11).
>
> By faith Moses' parents hid him (v. 23).
>
> By faith the people passed through the Red Sea (v. 29).

The writer of Hebrews goes on to describe the many positive, miraculous results of faith. But any reader who stops at verse 31 fails to see the total picture. Notice the following phrases compiled from verses 32-38: "Through faith . . . some faced jeers and flogging. . . . Others were tortured . . . stoned . . . sawed in two . . . put to death by the sword.... They went about destitute, persecuted and mistreated."

The saints suffered sorely by, through, and because of their faith.

God does not always paint reality as we would like it to be. If a person is suffering, it may be through faith. His or her affliction may not be a sign of weak faith, poor prayer habits, or a lack of maturity; it may be exactly the opposite. If God does not answer a prayer for the removal of sickness in the way we think it should be answered, God is still sovereign. God's sovereignty does not depend on our requests. His plan and sight are bigger than ours.

Does God heal? Yes, the Bible says God heals. (He healed Job!) Does God bless believers with success and financial victories? Yes, the Bible says God does. (Job died an old, rich man.) But if a person faces affliction, he or she may be facing it because of, or through, faith.

The Bible encourages us both to visit the sick and to pray "the prayer offered in faith" for the sick. God delivered Peter from prison, but He did not do the same for John the Baptist or for Peter the second time he was imprisoned. In the Old Testament, by faith, some crossed the Red Sea and, through faith, others died.

Until Jesus returns to earth, no miracle is truly completed. If a person is healed of brain cancer, he or she may still be subject to headaches and, of course, he or she will eventually die. We all face the deterioration of the body, a result of the Fall and its curse. Our skin will wrinkle, our hair will turn gray, our bones will weaken with age.

The Glory of God

The final issue is this. How, by faith, can we seek to see God glorified?

The person who develops a set of expectations excluding either side of the total picture makes improper demands on God, on others, on oneself. That person makes himself or herself the law and thereby judges others, may fail to express compassion, and falls into the sin of pride and idolatry.

An acquaintance of mine was dying of terminal cancer. For weeks, even months, the church to which he belonged prayed that God would heal him. But God chose not to intervene. In the midst of his suffering this young man's desire was to glorify Christ. Like Job's comforters, some Christians told him that he must have some secret sin. His parents carried heavy, embarrassed guilt for lacking faith. Yet their accusers never placed such platitudes on themselves.

I will never forget the words that cascaded from this friend's lips after a series of bombarding, accusing questions. He answered his accusers with great confidence, "God has been very good to me. I know I will be leaving this life soon. I know my date. My house is in order; I am ready to meet Jesus Christ face to face. Maybe you should pray for yourselves. You forget that you are terminal also. You just don't know your date."

Although his body was being destroyed, his perspective had been healed. Without the basic foundation of seeking to glorify God, we will lose perspective, live under unnecessary guilt, and be most susceptible to cultic groups. The desire to "glorify God in our bodies" will protect us, inoculate us against the poison of cults that stretch one part of God's truth to encompass the whole of their reality.

> Yes, and I will continue to rejoice, for I know that through your prayers and the help given by the Spirit of Jesus Christ, what has happened to me will turn out for

my deliverance. I eagerly expect and hope that I will in no way be ashamed, but will have sufficient courage so that now as always Christ will be exalted in my body, whether by life or by death. For to me, to live is Christ and to die is gain. If I am to go on living in the body, this will mean fruitful labor for me. Yet what shall I choose? I do not know! I am torn between the two: I desire to depart and be with Christ, which is better by far; but it is more necessary for you that I remain in the body. Convinced of this, I know that I will remain, and I will continue with all of you for your progress and joy in the faith, so that through my being with you again your joy in Christ Jesus will overflow on account of me (Philippians 1:18-26).

When he wrote these words, Paul was facing possible martyrdom. He did not condemn the Philippians for not "claiming faith" for his release. Paul only sought to glorify Jesus Christ.

10

The Many Paths to Spirituality

Many people describe our age as "apocalyptic"—an age in which everything will fall apart, a generation with no hope. We are disillusioned by the floods of corruption in government, economic crisis, religious shallowness, and superficial relationships. When floods of chaos engulf a society, when everything seems to be falling apart, people crave personal security. They are tempted to jump into any lifeboat that might keep them afloat.

Our generation is marked by broken families, abuse of minorities, the elderly and children, pressures of inflation, drugs, and the nuclear potential to annihilate all humanity. Seeing these raging waters, people attempt to cope by relating only to those they are sure of and understand.

At some time, we all fear the future. Among the couples I counsel for marriage, some have firmly decided not to have children. I always ask them why. Their main concern is always something deeper than overpopulation or the hunger crisis, but it is always based on a fear of the future. The thought of having children, spawning a future generation, forces us to crystallize our long-term hopes and goals.

The need for inner peace amid a fear of the future can drive people to the door of cults that offer immediate security, instant answers, support, and compassion.

Peter Marin has dubbed our times the age of the "new narcissism," a generation consumed in self-love. Speaking of a particular psychological cult, he states, "It is all so simple and straightforward. It has the terrifying simplicity of the lobotomized mind: all complexity gone, and in its place the warm wind of forced simplicity blowing away the tab ends of conscience and shame."[1]

Though blessed with tremendous affluence our Western culture is bankrupt in terms of the human relationships God ordained for the purpose of carrying us through life's difficulties. What does the increased enrollment in classes on communication skills and counseling as a profession tell us about our society? People long for relationships that will fill their needs for security and continuity. When this relational bankruptcy is coupled with the overstimulation of our emotions by the media, we become walking emotional vacuums, desperate for something or someone who will fill our void. Immediate self-fulfillment—whether through est, the New Age, the occult, Eastern religions, or some cult—becomes all-important. These groups seek to meet legitimate needs of an unglued age. They offer new experiences, lazy answers, meaningful encounters with other people, and an instantaneous structure for life.

Cultural Baggage

The struggles of the culture as a whole become a part of each of us. We as Christians cannot help but drag the baggage of the 1990s into our expectations of the church. The shallowness of life, the fear, and the call for immediate fulfillment are diseases that infect us all to some degree. Without knowing it, we may seek to fill the void and heal the disease of our age by trendy programs that give us a sense of meaning.

Instead of seeking renewal for our minds,

we often seek to patch them up by dividing life into small, easily defined compartments that we label "spiritual." Like many cult members, we long for simple "how-to" teachings on prayer, worship, evangelism, missions, social service, and family life. The final product: Christians running from speaker to seminar, looking for something to fill the hole in the center of their being.

When the inevitable pressures of life bear down on us, we are tempted to walk away discouraged or opt for a utopian land where we can cope. In their book *Being Human: The Nature of Spiritual Experience,* Ranald Macaulay and Jerram Barrs point out that two false views of spirituality have influenced the church throughout history. These teachings have led many into false religions and cults.

First, they describe the materialist view. Ours is a materialistic culture,

> a culture which denies the reality of God's existence. Because it denies the existence of God, it allows no possibility of the supernatural working in this world. There can be no relationship with God in the present, though psychological tech-

niques may be used to try to give
reality a "religious dimension."[2]

Unfortunately, many Christians unconscious-
ly think this way. For all practical purposes,
they live as if they were atheists. How? By failing to ask what difference the existence of God
makes in the way they handle finances, make
decisions on the job, face moral issues, and
order the overall agenda of their lives. Consider:
Do you expect God to intervene in your life
daily? What difference does your belief in God
make in the way you deal with other people,
figure your income taxes, solve your problems,
or treat people who are different from you?
When we fail to ask continually these basic
questions, we start viewing prayer as only a
psychological exercise by which we look for
instant relief. "Practical atheism" is a subtle
deception that can make us vulnerable to the
many cults that define religious experience only
in terms of psychological phenomena. They
offer emotional help, but discount the presence
of God in the daily workings of our lives.

Platonism
The other false view of spirituality that has
influenced many Christian groups and most
cults is Platonism.

In platonic thought the spiritual realm is considered superior to the material. The spirit is housed in a body of clay from which it longs to be released. Death gives that final release. In this life, however, the aim is to dwell in the realm of the spirit as far as possible... and deemphasize and devalue the material realm.[3]

Macaulay and Barrs explain this view and its consequences. From the time of Christ to today, Platonism has had tremendous influence in the church. It is the core of the basic beliefs and teachings of most cults.

What did Plato teach? Basically, that the body is bad and the spirit good. Both the biblical and the Platonic views are different from the materialist view, which denies the spiritual realms of reality. But biblical Christianity differs from Platonism in that Christianity does not present the body as a prison of the immortal soul.

The Bible begins by stating that Someone existed before the Creation. This Person, God, is the all-powerful, sovereign sustainer of the universe. God created the material world and saw it as good, not a prison. Human beings are created in the image of the Creator. All that God created was perfect. At a certain point in history, humanity chose to rebel against God. This revolt did not change the faculties of humanness. People are still rational and reasonable, but they pollute these faculties. People are still aesthetic; they still enjoy beauty. They can still experience and enjoy love, but this, like every other aspect of life on earth, is marred by the effects of the revolt.

In the Bible, redemption is seen in light of Creation. Unfortunately some views of Christian growth and spirituality neglect this biblical foundation. As a result they teach a concept of spirituality similar to that of the cults. Ask yourself, What are Christians being redeemed from? Many Christians are asserting and living a denial of life rather than an affirmation of life as God created life to be lived.

The Bible teaches the resurrection of the body, not the immortality of the soul. The Bible places a high value on creation. Jesus Christ became flesh. Christ ate and slept, and He bled when His hands were pierced. He experienced all the aspects of being physical, as God so intends for all of us.

The Platonic view of spirituality held by

many cults and some Christians sees redemption as only a "spiritual" problem. The concept is a subtle one. How often have you said, "Jesus wants to come into your hearts"? Do you think in terms of Jesus saving only "souls"? If so, you may have adopted a cultic concept. The Bible teaches that Jesus Christ wants people in totality—a person's body, family life, thoughts, relationships with others and with the state and with the church. Every aspect of living in our bodies is to be lived before God in thanksgiving. God's plan of redemption is not just futuristic, but includes the process of redemption now.

This is portrayed clearly by Paul in his letter to Christians in Rome. For eleven chapters Paul focuses on doctrine: God's sovereign grace, humanity's sinfulness, and Christ's redeeming work in history. Just before Paul goes on to discuss Christian living (ethics), he uses the word *bodies*.

> Therefore, I urge you, brothers, in view of God's mercy, to offer your bodies as living sacrifices, holy and pleasing to God—which is your spiritual worship. Do not conform any longer to the pattern of this

world, but be transformed by the
renewing of your mind. Then you
will be able to test and approve what
God's will is—his good, pleasing
and perfect will (Romans 12:1-2).

Paul reminds us here of the mercy of God. In
this context Paul uses this first-century "nonre-
ligious" word *body*. Paul asks these Christians
to present their total selves—not just their
"hearts" or spirits—to God as a living sacrifice.

Sacrifices were common to the great mystery religions and to Old Testament believers.
All these sacrifices involved the killing of a
body, but Paul says God wants a living body.

Religious people love to give spiritual sacrifices to win God's favor. But spiritual ecstasy
is the only reward for giving only of one's
inner self. Fighting the false religions of his
day, Paul defines spirituality in terms of our
presenting our total selves, including our bodies, to God.

First Corinthians 6:20 tells us to honor God
with our bodies. Paul uses this term *body* to
refer, in positive terms, to the total person. In
much the same manner he uses the term "flesh"
(KJV) or 'sinful nature" (NIV) to symbolize, in
negative terms, our sinful nature (Romans 8:5).

The Platonic view calls people to be "spiritual." It sounds right, but how does it differ from the biblical view? The Bible insists that our problem is moral rebellion against God. For the Christian, salvation is not a denial of one's humanity, but a recognition of sin and acceptance of Jesus Christ as one's Savior. This acceptance enables us to glorify God in our bodies, as intended before the Fall. The final goal, then, is to live now under the authority of God's Word, free from guilt, redeeming all of life.

The Bible views the body in a positive way. Regrettably, many Christians view the body as distasteful, unspiritual, and something to be rejected. Such a view of spirituality is similar to many major cults.

> Ultimately we hope to overcome our bodies or escape them; then we will be like Christ, we think. In this view bodily pleasure is especially suspect.... Sleeping, eating, drinking, going to the bathroom, making love, combing our hair, and putting on makeup may be the activity of bodies, and may consume a good portion of our day, but

these activities are seen as irrele-
vant to or a hindrance to seeking
first the kingdom of God.[4]

Paul says that if we want to do something
religious or spiritual, we should give our bodies to God. The New Testament does not view
the body as a thing to be crushed so that the
spirit can be released. The spiritual act will
not be the burning of incense, the pinching of
salt, the waiting for a lineup of the planets, or a
searching for the right mood. It will simply be
the presenting of one's entire self to God, giving back to Him what He gave us in creation.

Biblical spirituality and Christian worship
begin with this act. The Platonists and the
cults of the first century would have viewed
Romans 12:1-2 as anti-religious, distasteful,
and unspiritual. So far as they were concerned, the body was evil and God wanted
nothing to do with it. For them the call was to
get out of body and mind and into the spirit.

The great mysteries of the Christian faith
are the Incarnation, God becoming flesh, having hinged thumbs and toes, expanding lungs,
a valved heart, and a digestive system, God as
man being crucified and then restored in the
Resurrection.

In the beginning was the Word, and the Word was with God, and the Word was God. He was with God in the beginning. Through him all things were made; without him nothing was made that has been made.

In him was life, and that life was the light of men. The light shines in the darkness, but the darkness has not understood it....

He was in the world, and though the world was made through him, the world did not recognize him. He came to that which was his own, but his own did not receive him. Yet to all who received him, to those who believed in his name, he gave the right to become children of God—children born not of natural descent, nor of human decision or a husband's will, but born of God.

The Word became flesh and lived for a while among us. We have seen his glory, the glory of the one and only Son, who came from the Father, full of grace and truth (John 1 1-5, 10-14).

Jesus Christ, the Word, was raised from the dead; a physical, material being was lifted into the Godhead. If we depreciate our bodies, we depreciate the very vehicle God uses to accomplish His work, which is our sanctification (our becoming more Christlike in character) and our service to others. In an article, "Any Body Can be Spiritual," Bert H. Hodges writes,

> The Incarnation was a very physical affair. It involved the birth of a baby.... Jesus went to a wedding... touched people... healed their sicknesses ate meals....
>
> The physicalness of the Incarnation is so blatant that it embarrasses us as "spiritual" Christians. We wish the Incarnation were somehow a more pristine, mystical affair. That God became body and lived in this mundane, fallen world where one must be concerned with dressing, eating, sleeping, sexuality and the effects of sin on these activities is too mysterious.[5]

Paul saw the giving of our bodies as the apex of spirituality. Why? So that we might test, through experience, the will of God. In this aspect, the will of God is the same for all. "Spiritual worship," the giving of our bodies and minds, is the key to discovering that God's will is good, squares with reality, is acceptable, and brings maturity and wholeness. God's will is not some nebulous mystical formula; it involves giving our minds and bodies to God so that we can live to God's glory.

The apostle uses the language of laypeople and amateurs. Those who speak religious expert-ese would cringe at the use of the words *bodies* and *minds,* but these two words should not be taken lightly. The body and mind are the focal point of the Book of Romans, the transition between doctrine (teaching) and practice (living). The rest of Paul's letter gives instruction regarding one's responsibility to family, neighbors, and the state.

Paul doesn't say, "Give yourselves when you become holy." Neither does he ask believers to present their hearts, souls, or spirits to God—that would be too easy! He says we must give our created, concrete selves, with all our fears, doubts, problems, abilities, gifts, dreams, and hopes. Give your problematic self to God. That is spirituality.

Not All Bliss

Lest we be naive, we must note that Paul informs believers of an immediate crisis: There will be a tension between the passing idols of each age and God's values (Romans 12:2). This tension cannot be avoided, regardless of how "spiritual" we may become. Paul urges believers to call the bluff of all such fads.

This concept of spirituality will greatly influence whether we confront or run from the various crises brought by living in a world affected by the Fall.

Faith in this context is a good discovery. Faith does not negate our humanity. It is, in the words of Ranald Macaulay and Jerram Barrs, an "affirmation of life." To be human is to be in the image of God.

Paul says that God's love triggers our faith. False religions and cults claim that our increased faith will increase God's love for us, but actually our faith does not influence God's love. Because of God's mercy, love, and grace, we can and should trust Jesus Christ with our total being. When we keep this foremost in our minds, we are immune to the false teaching that only certain people can be spiritual. The Bible does not call us to have great faith in God, but faith in a great God!

Giving one's total self is essential to understanding and discerning the deception and bluff of cults.

Why Renew the Mind?

We must not assume that only pastors, leaders, or counselors can have renewed minds. The Holy Spirit can renew any believer's mind in concrete ways.

A renewed mind is critical for discerning false teaching in the church and in cults. Many Christians are calling for us to get out of the mind and into the spirit, but doing so may prove dangerous. This aspect of our humanity is God's major weapon to protect us from false teachings and cults.

In his book *Your Mind Matters,* John R .W. Stott states, "Nobody wants a cold, joyless, intellectual Christianity."[6] How true! But Stott explains that a Christian's battle against the forces of evil is a battle of the mind, a battle of ideas.

Note Paul's references to maturity, discernment, and Christian living in the following passages. They are found in a mind when Jesus Christ is its Lord.

> The weapons we fight with are not
> the weapons of the world. On the

contrary, they have divine power to demolish strongholds. We demolish arguments and every pretension that sets itself up against the knowledge of God, and we take captive every thought to make it obedient to Christ. And we will be ready to punish every act of disobedience, once your obedience is complete (2 Corinthians 10:4-6).

Finally, brothers, whatever is true, whatever is noble, whatever is right, whatever is pure, whatever is lovely, whatever is admirable—if anything is excellent or praiseworthy—think about such things. Whatever you have learned or received or heard from me, or seen in me—put it into practice. And the God of peace will be with you (Philippians 4:8-9).

Both passages say our thoughts—our renewed minds—safeguard us against deception. A mind "not renewed" is a mind vulnerable to cults and false teaching.

How Do We Judge a False Teacher?

How are we to judge prophets? On the spiritual feeling we receive in our spirits? No! On the content of their message.

> The Spirit clearly says that in later times some will abandon the faith and follow deceiving spirits and things taught by demons. Such teachings come through hypocritical liars, whose consciences have been seared as with a hot iron. They forbid people to marry and order them to abstain from certain foods, which God created to be received with thanksgiving by those who believe and who know the truth (I Timothy 4: 1-4).

False teachers, even those who call themselves Christians, will always despise creation. They will present a higher, legalistic spirituality. Creation for the believer has been sanctified and consecrated by God; it is to be received with gratitude. Note Paul's words: "For everything God created is good, and nothing is to be rejected if it is received with thanksgiving, because it is consecrated by the word of God and prayer" (I Timothy 4:4-5).

John also warns the church of false teachers. Does he encourage them to judge a teacher by the feelings of spirituality given off? No. Again, our minds must examine the content of a teacher's message, noticing what is said about Jesus Christ having come in a physical body.

> Dear friends, do not believe every spirit, but test the spirits to see whether they are from God, because many false prophets have gone out into the world. This is how you can recognize the Spirit of God: Every spirit that acknowledges that Jesus Christ has come in the flesh is from God, but every spirit that does not acknowledge Jesus is not from God. This is the spirit of the antichrist, which you have heard is coming and even now is already in the world (I John 4:1-3).

To judge the spirituality of pastors, speakers, Sunday school teachers, and evangelists on the amount of emotion they exude or stir up is wrong and dangerous. The movie *Deceived* recalls many People's Temple services in which persons shared needs, gave testimonies, and praised God with great excitement. But they were deceived; the depth of their emotion and excitement was not founded in the discovery of God's love through Jesus Christ. The knowledge of Christ will lead to true worship, faith, holiness, and love (see Romans 11:33; Luke 24:32; John 13:17).

The Holy Spirit can renew anyone's mind. A Ph.D. is not a prerequisite for being able to discern and thus be protected from deception. A mind renewed by God's Spirit and the knowledge of Scripture is available to all believers who concern themselves with prayer, faith, study, reflection, and personal commitment to Christ's lordship. The minds given to us by God in creation are integral and crucial to our spirituality. Minds renewed are minds protected from deception, fraud, and manipulation. If in our minds we think we are not susceptible to cults, we are most vulnerable.

11

Please Don't Water the Garden

A Boston television station produced a series of programs on the land of Egypt and its history. One of these programs focused on the treasures discovered in the ancient tombs. Among these finds were some grains of wheat. The archaeologists planted these seeds, which had been entombed for several thousand years, in rich soil. They were watered and given sunlight, and to everyone's amazement, they grew.

Christians often think that the seeds of heresy are found only in cults and in offbeat sects of Christianity. But John, in his first letter, and Paul, in his letter to the Ephesians, remind us that heretical teachers are often found within the church itself. Jesus notes that the dormant seeds of unorthodoxy can be buried in the lawns of the church. In Matthew 13, Jesus tells a parable of the kingdom of heaven: The enemy sowed seeds within this kingdom. In our desire to discover and understand the doctrines of cults, we may forget that potential gardens of heresy lie within our own walls. Remember: Sun Myung Moon was raised a Presbyterian; David Berg, founder of the Children of God, was once an Evangelical pastor; Jim Jones pastored a Christian church; many leaders in the People's Temple and Jonestown were former members of Nazarene, Roman Catholic, Baptist, Methodist, and Assemblies of God churches.

Under the right circumstances we are all capable of watering the seeds of false teaching that lie dormant in the church itself. Without even realizing what they are doing, pastors can water these gardens. Congregations can unwittingly build greenhouses. Parachurch organizations can make the "spring rains" fall. And individuals can add the nutrients that cause these plants to flourish and ripen, to become ready for harvest.

How Can Pastors Water the Garden?

Pastors can water the seedbeds of falsehood by projecting the image that their lives are altogether and free from struggles and weaknesses. When this happens, they invite unhealthy loyalties into the congregation.

God often matches congregations with pastors for mutual ministry. The word *ministry* implies giving help. Mutual ministry implies that both the pastor and the congregation have needs to be met by the other. The congregation may be strong in qualities where the pastor is weak, and vice versa. This kind of ministry of growth involves continual self-evaluation, prayer, thought, and serious study of God's Word. A constant willingness by both pastor and congregation to be open to instruction— from God's Word, from mutual confrontation, and from prayer for each other—will deter exploitation.

Pastors water the seeds of heresy when they spend the majority of their time in administration rather than in consistent prayer, in Bible study, and in ministry to their congregations. Pastors may encourage congregations to build unhealthy images of the pastoral ministry when they live as though their higher calling is free from struggle and weaknesses.

Pastors and leaders need to know their personal limitations. There is a danger in confusing the role of pastor with that of a professional counselor. Counseling demands have led many pastors to exhaustion; with only twenty-four hours in the day, they have had to lower the quality of their teaching, preaching, and time for prayer. Some have become so discouraged, they have left the ministry. A pastor's primary call is to teach God's Word, to pray, and to minister to the congregation. Of course, this will involve some counseling; involvement with and concern for people's needs must not be avoided, for this was the model of Christ. But not admitting our counseling limitations can produce some tragic results. We may create an unhealthy dependence for members of our congregation, which may further result in unhealthy and misaligned affections.

Personally I see the need to protect myself from long-term counseling relationships. As a rule, I allow only a few counseling sessions per problem. After three sessions I evaluate the situation and decide: Will I continue, or direct the person to professional help? This gives me freedom to place checks and balances on myself and avoid unhealthy emotional attachments or dependencies. At this juncture I often direct the person to a professional counselor, a Bible study group, or another group designed to meet his or her specific need. This evaluation point also protects me from yielding to any temptation to meet my own egoistic needs by building unhealthy, overdependent loyalties.

As pastors and teachers we can also water the seeds of heresy when we fail to keep in mind the biblical goals of discipling. Our goal should be to help move those who look to us for guidance toward growth and development that is separate from us. The Book of Acts presents a unique picture of a healthy, helping, discipling relationship. Soon after Paul's conversion, Barnabas took Paul under his care, helping him to develop as a church leader. The first references to the pair speak of "Barnabas and Paul." But later the writer of Acts shifts the relationship to "Paul and Barnabas," and eventually the focus is only on Paul. We water heretical seeds when we fail to encourage those under our care to continue their development, perhaps even beyond our own.

This model of discipling and teaching is unique, healthful, and successful. Barnabas was concerned that Paul develop his own skills, style, and abilities, that he move out of a dependent relationship into a more personally fulfilled ministry.

Churches Can Build Greenhouses

Without even realizing it, Christian churches can build the walls of a greenhouse in which cultic tendencies flourish, in which seedlings sprout, and from where they can be transplanted into someone else's garden. What material do we use for the studs and beams of these greenhouses? What kind of solar panels do we use? What auxiliary heat do we employ?

We pour the foundation and put up the studs when we build a total ministry around one personality. There should be a sense of excitement about what God is doing in many American "superchurches." Many of these large congregations enjoy continuing growth and creative ministries. But a pattern shared by many of these churches needs to be checked: At first the pastor preaches good sermons with good biblical examples, causing crowds to come. Before long, the church hosts a nationwide radio program, a cassette ministry, and perhaps a television ministry. The pastor is soon marketed Madison Avenue-style, and in time the superchurch becomes marked with its own trendy clichés. Often the demands of the pastorate become so great that sermon content begins to take second place to other responsibilities.

Listen to the message presented in your church. Be ever grateful for what God has accomplished, but ask yourself whether, over the years, biblical content has given way to stories or fads of the decade. Take a pen and paper and note the amount of time spent on raising money, dealing with issues, story telling, and solid biblical instruction with practical application.

Congregations build these greenhouses when they allow themselves to be enamored by success without ever examining the possible subtle flaws in the church structure or teaching.

We water the little seeds of heresy in new converts when we continually talk about the pastor of our church, rather than about Jesus Christ. These seeds can easily sprout and then be transplanted into another garden, maybe that of some new personality cult.

Churches install the solar panels and lights that encourage the growth of heresy when their ministry is centered around only one aspect of the gospel, thus neglecting the whole counsel of God. They might teach only the ministry of the Holy Spirit or evangelism, for example. A fragmented perspective on Scripture will nourish the dormant seeds that lie waiting for conditions conducive to life. In this kind of church, members are often not free to discern from the whole counsel of God, the preaching of which would help entomb heresy.

We nourish false teaching when we have unrealistic and unbiblical expectations of what the church should be. We nourish the sprouts of heresy when we get more excited about hearing stories than about the biblical truths they illustrate.

Congregations are often guilty of putting their pastors in a bind, expecting them to spend a majority of time in administration rather than in ministry or Bible study and prayer. Such unbiblical demands can cause the best of pastors to veer off track, to succumb to unbiblical priorities.

Organizations that Water the Soil

During the past few decades, many para-church ministries have been born. They have been responsible for the conversion of many, yet are all these groups really just an arm of the church, as they claim? Many pastors who have worked close to the central offices of parachurch organizations can tell a string of tragic stories about burned-out leaders and the rubble of the families of those who have given their lives for the cause. They can describe families who are not involved in a local church because of the pressures of their ministry.

We need to ask ourselves: Are the parachurch ministries really a functioning arm of the church or an arm severed? To whom are such organizations accountable? When we accept their ministries without questioning their accountability, their view of the church, or their handling of finances, we prepare the way for seeds of deception to grow.

Parachurch organizations, including what is called the "electronic church," water the seeds of heresy when they define themselves in opposition to the local church, all the while coaxing (without accountability) money from the local church members.

On one occasion I was invited by a national parachurch youth organization to speak at a high school. The speaker before me spent fifteen minutes explaining how his organization, disillusioned with the church, identified with the student's rejection of the institution. I was then introduced as a pastor from a local church! These incongruous messages can not help but confuse the people who hear them. Such messages turn people against the very institution God ordained to be their help. I felt compelled to discuss my reactions with the speaker. I thank God we agreed to help each other's ministry. Our parish developed a training program for their leaders, and they directed new converts to us to become established in a local church.

Another problem is that a parachurch organization can be orthodox in doctrine, yet function like a cult in issues of authority and abuse of power.

While living in Europe, my wife and I were involved with an Evangelical youth mission based in Switzerland. We were with the group only six weeks, but it was almost seven years before I had overcome the psychological damage caused by their cult-like control and spiritualization.

Upon arrival at the headquarters each team member was given a "victory sheet," which instructed him or her never to question those in leadership and never to write home any negative comments. Questioning a leader was considered an act of rebellion against God and His chain of command. Team members were kept constantly busy, even overextended, for the cause. Married partners were separated from each other. All the organization's demands were adhered to for the sake of "spirituality." When some of us grew tired, causing tempers to shrink, those in authority pointed out how sinful we were and how much we needed to depend on those in spiritual authority over us. Any of us who raised questions regarding the stewardship of our bodies were suddenly branded as being "in the flesh." Any who questioned exaggerated stories of miracles, finances, or poor diets were accused of bringing sin into the camp.

When I think of this group and other parachurch groups who value authority and uniformity, I recall the words of Ronald Enroth:

> In strongly authoritarian movements or churches, those who persist in raising uncomfortable questions, especially after they have left the group, are labeled "reprobates" or worse yet, "agents of Satan." The weak and the meek who have legitimate concerns and questions do not dare to share those reservations, sometimes because of group pressure, sometimes because they have been subjected to control mechanisms of fear, guilt, and spiritual intimidation.[1]

Although the group I was in was thoroughly Christian in doctrine and in motive, they were blind to the manipulative controls being placed on team members. How tragic that some who left the team have rejected not only the para-church organization, but the church and Christ. They still have not fully recovered.

We need to remember that people who have been burned by questionable tactics of a para-church group or a church may heal very slowly. This is pointed out by James and Marcia Rudin. In their book *Prison or Paradise?* they show that it can take years to overcome the fears and psychological damage incurred in a cultic group. Personal experience has shown me that it can take years for a victim to stabilize, learn to trust others, and to build healthy rela-tionships. People often need professional help beyond what a pastor or church is able to give.

Parachurch organizations can sow dishon-esty when they use tricky means to hide their evangelistic agendas. Questions about integri-ty should be asked when evangelism cam-paigns are launched under the guise of "church surveys." What is the difference between these surveys and the computerized surveys used by some of the leading cults to lure converts? Surely there is no difference in tactic.

Parachurch groups cultivate the seeds of cultism and heresy when they claim to offer more than the church rather than claiming to be a supporting arm of the church. I recently attended a meeting of Christians where the speaker was the host of a popular Christian television talk program. I took note of one particular sentence: "Most church services are boring and most TV church services are boring." Immediately the audience broke into applause. In a sense, they were applauding the seeds of heresy. They were revealing their misunderstanding of the nature, purpose, and mission of the church and worship. We reveal our worldliness when we come to church expecting worship to be another "Sesame Street" explosion of entertainment. When we rate a worship service only on its level of excitement, we border on being deceived by the bizarre—that which will delight, dazzle, and entertain. The political rallies of Nazis at Nuremberg were filled with liturgical life modeled after Benedictine liturgy. The services of the People's Temple were characterized by joyful, excited expressions of testimony and songs of praise; their delight had nothing to do with biblical Christianity.

Certainly the discipline of going to worship can be boring. Weekly confession of our sins to God can also be boring. Who likes to get on their knees and worship God or discipline their minds to hear God's Word or acknowledge that God only is God? We make the ground ready for cult leaders to sow the seeds of heresy when we follow the world in thinking that life, including worship, should be only thrills.

Weed Killer Alone Will Not Do the Job

There will always be some seeds of heresy lying buried in the church. We are deceived if we think that right doctrine alone is the weed killer that will destroy them forever.

John, the beloved disciple, addressed this problem in his writings to the early church. John was with Christ throughout His ministry. They were close friends. Jesus entrusted His mother to John's care. John witnessed the birth of the church and was one of its founding leaders. But at the close of his life, wrinkled by age, John saw the need to challenge the seeds of heresy within the church. Note the power of his words:

> Dear children, this is the last hour;
> and as you have heard that the
> antichrist is coming, even now
> many antichrists have come. This
> is how we know it is the last hour.

> They went out from us, but they did
> not really belong to us. For if they
> had belonged to us, they would
> have remained with us; but their
> going showed that none of them
> belonged to us.
>
> But you have an anointing from the
> Holy One, and all of you know the
> truth. I do not write to you because
> you do not know the truth, but
> because you do know it and because
> no lie comes from the truth. Who is
> the liar? It is the man who denies
> that Jesus is the Christ. Such a man
> is the antichrist—he denies the
> Father and the Son (I John 2:18-22).

The ultimate deceiver, the ultimate cult
leader, will be the Antichrist, but this letter
was written to Christians, not to members of
some crazy cult. John makes it clear that the
seeds of heresy are in our hearts. When we
deny that Jesus Christ is Lord we are, in spirit,
the Antichrist.

When do we deny Christ? When we willfully continue to do what we know is wrong.
Seeds of heresy are nourished when we willfully harbor bitterness, prejudice, and an

unforgiving spirit. We may be doctrinally sound, but if we in practice willfully reject God's Word, we deny Christ. So John continues his letter by encouraging us to practice the Christian life. Many people never lose their faith—they just fail to shape their lives by it. Behavior unchecked, attitudes not dealt with, resentments harbored—all cause us to build up beliefs that justify our immaturity and irresponsible behavior.

Even after having several children, husbands or wives have told me that their marriages were "out of the will of God" and therefore they were going to leave their families. I even listened as one woman involved in a questionable group told me that after much prayer, the Holy Spirit had led her to Paul's words, "Put on the new man." She took the "word" as telling her to leave her husband for someone else. Though this particular situation is extreme, isn't it, in principle, how we rationalize many of our actions? John continues his instruction in his letter by listing safeguards that protect us from this subtle deception. John's counsel can be summarized in two words: obedience and service.

> And now, dear children, continue in
> him, so that when he appears we

may be confident and unashamed before him at his coming.

If you know that he is righteous, you know that everyone who does what is right has been born of him.

How great is the love the Father has lavished on us, that we should be called children of God! And that is what we are! The reason the world does not know us is that it did not know him. Dear friends, now we are children of God, and what we will be has not yet been made known. But we know that when he appears, we shall be like him, for we shall see him as he is. Everyone who has this hope in him purifies himself, just as he is pure.

Everyone who sins breaks the law; in fact, sin is lawlessness. But you know that he appeared so that he might take away our sins. And in him is no sin. No one who lives in him keeps on sinning. No one who continues to sin has either seen him or known him.

Dear children, do not let anyone

lead you astray. He who does what is right is righteous, just as he is righteous. He who does what is sinful is of the devil, because the devil has been sinning from the beginning. The reason the Son of God appeared was to destroy the devil's work. No one who is born of God will continue to sin, because God's seed remains in him; he cannot go on sinning, because he has been born of God. This is how we know who the children of God are and who the children of the devil are: Anyone who does not do what is right is not a child of God neither is anyone who does not love his brother (I John 2:28-3:10).

If we are to be alert to these issues of self-deception and manipulation by others—the pitfalls of denying Christ—we must earnestly pray, study the Word, examine ourselves, and honestly reflect upon the whole counsel of God. We need to know both our strengths and our weaknesses. We must guard those areas where we know we are most tempted to manipulate others or to allow them to manipu-

late us. We are all sinful. To think otherwise
is to deceive ourselves. Remember that the
warning "If we claim to be without sin, we
deceive ourselves and the truth is not in us" (I
John 1:8) was written to Christians—not unbelievers or cult members!

Each of us must examine past relationships
and see whether there have been certain patterns of behavior and needs that have caused
us to use others or allowed them to exploit us.
We must stand against those weaknesses and
pray with others that God will protect us in the
future from such pitfalls.

There is something more dangerous in life
than being wrong: being right. When fighting
for truth and against false teaching, we can
easily be blind to our own vulnerability. In this
blindness we attack the colossal and scandalous
faults and mistakes of others without routing
our own sins that are just as big and ugly.
God's grace frees us to be open with Him and
to install checks and balances in our lives.
When we place such controls on ourselves, we
are less apt to place controls on others.

Apart from Christology, John's letter concerning heresy says little about the nature and
teaching of false teachers. He did remind
those first-century believers, and Christians

throughout history, that we can all play an unwitting part in allowing the seeds of heresy to grow; we can all plow the ground, plant the seeds, nourish them, build a hothouse, or prepare the sprouts for transplanting.

This old man, this friend of Christ, was concerned that the seeds remain as dormant as those wheat seeds that were sealed inside the Egyptian pyramid. John was concerned that none of us be guilty of watering the garden.

Notes

Bibliography

Notes

Chapter 1

[1]John Moriconi, *Children of God, Family of Love* (Downers Grove, IL: InterVarsity Press, 1980).

Chapter 3

[1]Ronald Enroth, *Youth, Brainwashing and the Extremist Cults* (Grand Rapids: Zondervan, 1977), p. 208.

[2]Ibid., p. 203.

[3]Mel White, *Deceived* (Old Tappan, NJ.: Fleming H. Revell, 1979), p. 231.

[4]Stephen B. Clark, *Man and Woman in Christ* (Ann Arbor, MI: Servant Books, 1980), p. 360.

[5]Ibid.

[6]Charles Farah, Jr., "A Critical Analysis: The 'Roots and Fruits' of Faith-Formula Theology," in *Pneuma: The Journal of the Society for Pentecostal Studies* (Spring 1981): p. 15.

[7]See discussion of this in Farah, "A Critical Analysis," p. 17.

[8]A. James Rudin and Marcia R. Rudin, *Prison or Paradise? The New Religious Cults* (Philadelphia: Fortress Press, 1980), p. 23.

[9]Michael Griffiths, *Unsplitting Your Christian Life* (Downers Grove, IL: InterVarsity Press, 1971), p. 22.

[10]Ibid., p. 23.

[11]Ibid., p. 25

Chapter 4

[1]"Congressional Report Recommends Actions As Result of Jonestown Tragedy," in *The Advisor: Journal of the American Family Foundation* 1, no. I (August 1979):2: Citing the report entitled "The Assassination of Representative Leo T. Ryan and the Jonestown, Guyana Tragedy," U.S. Govt. Printing Office (15 May 1979).

[2]Curtis Hartman, with Ann Rodgers and Tom Morton, "God for the 'Up and Out,'" in *Boston* 73, no. 5 (May 1981):143.

[3]Ibid., p. 188.

Chapter 5

[1]Dietrich Bonhoeffer, *Life Together* (New York: Harper & Row, 1954), pp. 27-28.

Chapter 6

[1]Lucille Lavender, *They Cry, Too!* (Wheaton, IL: Tyndale House Publishers, 1979) .

[2]Ronald M. Enroth, "Door Interview," in the *Wittenburg Door* 59 (February-March 1981):14.

[3]Ronald M. Enroth, "The Power Abusers," in *Eternity* (October 1979) :23.

[4]Ibid., p. 24.

[5]Paul Tournier, *The Violence Within,* trans. Edwin Hudson (San Francisco: Harper & Row, 1978), p. 148.

[6]Ben Patterson, "Don Quixote and the Cults," Editorial, in the *Wittenburg Door* 59 (February-March 1981):5.

[7]Steven W. Larson, "And a Little Child Shall Lead Them" (Unpublished college text, Gordon College, Wenham, MA, 1980), p. 23.

Chapter 9

[1]James W. Sire, *Scripture Twisting: 20 Ways the Cults Misread the Bible* (Downers Grove, IL: InterVarsity Press, 1980). This is one of the best books available for helping Christians to understand a basic approach to biblical interpretation.

[2]Gordon D. Fee, *The Disease of the Health and Wealth Gospels* (Costa Mesa, CA: The

Word for Today, n.d.). These essays originally appeared in *Agora* magazine in 1979.

Chapter 10

[1]Peter Marin, "The New Narcissism," in *Harper's* magazine (October 1975) :46.

[2]Ranald Macaulay and Jerram Barrs, *Being Human: The Nature of Spiritual Experience* (Downers Grove, IL: InterVarsity Press, 1978) p. 30.

[3]Ibid., p. 43.

[4]Bert H. Hodges, "Any Body Can Be Spiritual," in the *Gordon Alumnus* 11, no. 1 (Summer 1981):23.

[5]Ibid., pp. 23-24.

[6]John R.W. Stott, *Your Mind Matters: The Place of the Mind in the Christian Life* (Downers Grove, IL: InterVarsity Press, 1973), p. 1.

Chapter 11

[1]Enroth, "The Power Abusers."

Bibliography

The Advisor: Journal of the American Family Foundation, August 1979.

Augsburger, David. *Caring Enough to Confront.* Glendale, CA: Regal Books, 1974.

Berghoef, Gerard, and De Koster, Lester. *The Elders Handbook: A Practical Guide for Church Leaders.* Grand Rapids: Christian's Library Press, 1979.

Bonhoeffer, Dietrich. *Life Together.* New York: Harper & Row, 1954

Clark, Stephen B. *Man and Woman in Christ.* Ann Arbor: Servant Books, 1980.

Collins, Gary. *People Helper Growthbook.* Santa Ana, CA: Vision House, 1979.

Dodds, E. R. *Pagan and Christian in an Age of Anxiety.* New York: W. W. Norton, 1965.

Enroth, Ronald M. "The Power Abusers." *Eternity,* October 1979, p. 22.

_____. "Door Interview." *Wittenburg Door,* February-March 1981, pp. 14-15.

_____. *Youth, Brainwashing and the Extremist Cults.* Grand Rapids: Zondervan, 1977.

Farah, Charles, Jr. "A Critical Analysis: The 'Roots and Fruits' of Faith-Formula Theology." *Pneuma: The Journal of the Society for Pentecostal Studies,* Spring 1981, pp. 3-21.

Fee, Gordon D. *The Disease of the Health and Wealth Gospels.* Costa Mesa, CA: The Word for Today, n.d.

Griffiths, Michael. *Unsplitting Your Christian Life.* Downers Grove, IL: InterVarsity Press, 1971.

Hartman, Curtis et al. "God for the 'Up and Out.'" *Boston,* May 1981, p. 142.

Hodges, Bert H. "Any Body Can Be Spiritual." *Gordon Alumnus,* Summer 1981, pp. 21-24.

Larson, Steven W. "And a Little Child Shall Lead Them: A Brief Study of Power, Leadership, and Servanthood." Unpublished course text, Gordon College, Wenham, MA, 1980.

Lavender, Lucille. *They Cry, Too!* Wheaton, IL: Tyndale House Publishers, 1979.

Macaulay, Ranald, and Barrs, Jerram. *Being Human: The Nature of Spiritual Experience.* Downers Grove, IL: InterVarsity Press, 1978.

Marin, Peter. "The New Narcissism." *Harper's* magazine, October 1975.

Martin, Walter R. *The Kingdom of the Cults.* Rev. ed. Minneapolis: Bethany Fellowship, 1968.

Moriconi, John. *Children of God, Family of Love.* Downers Grove, IL: InterVarsity Press, 1980.

Patterson, Ben. "Don Quixote and the Cults." *Wittenburg Door,* February-March 1981, p. 3.

Rudin, A. James, and Rudin, Marcia R. *Prison or Paradise? The New Religious Cults.* Philadelphia: Fortress Press, 1980.

Schaeffer, Edith. *Affliction.* Old Tappan, NJ.: Fleming H. Revell, 1978.

Sire, James W. *Scripture Twisting: 20 Ways the Cults Misread the Bible.* Downers Grove, IL: InterVarsity Press, 1980.

Sproul, R. C. *Knowing Scripture.* Downers Grove, IL: InterVarsity Press, 1977.

Stedman, Ray C. *Body Life.* Glendale, CA: Regal Books, 1972.

Stott, John R. W. *Your Mind Matters: The Place of the Mind in the Christian Life.* Downers Grove, IL: InterVarsity Press, 1973.

Tournier, Paul. *The Violence Within.* Translated by Edwin Hudson. San Francisco: Harper & Row, 1978.

White, Mel. *Deceived.* Old Tappan, NJ: Fleming H. Revell, Spire Books, 1979.

Wise, Robert L. *When There Is No Miracle.* Glendale, CA: Regal Books, 1977.

Yamamoto, J. Isamu. *The Moon Doctrine.* 2nd ed. Downers Grove, IL: InterVarsity Press, 1977.

About the Author

HAROLD L. BUSSÉLL is Dean of the Chapel at Gordon College. He holds degrees from Bethany Bible College (B.A.), the University of Santa Clara (M.A. in counseling psychology), and Andover-Newton Theological Seminary (D. Min.). He is a former pastor and has worked with Teen Challenge in Europe.

chapter one

When Shawn Quincy rushed into the sitting room with the news that a cast member of "The Rich Game" had been found dead in bed upstairs, Brenda almost choked on her coffee. As a talented ballet dancer and actor, Shawn had often told stories that made her sides ache with laughter. But Brenda could see by the look on his face that this time his news was real. The owner of the Sheffield Bed and Breakfast quickly set down her coffee and sprinted up the stairs to the room Shawn had pointed out to her.

Breathing hard, Brenda stepped cautiously into the room just long enough to see a body lying unnaturally still atop the quilt. She closed her eyes for a brief moment, then stepped back into the hall.

As she ushered a few curious guests and staff members away and prepared to call the authorities, she realized that the cherished serenity of the Sheffield Bed and Breakfast was about to change.

The Sheffield Bed and Breakfast, a stately, historic Queen Anne-style mansion that boasted gorgeous flower gardens and a sweeping view of the Atlantic Ocean, was a beloved institution in the seaside town of Sweetfern Harbor. Its guests returned year after year, drawn to its charms, but also, perhaps, to its mysteries.

Prior to that fateful morning, Brenda had been enjoying a successful summer season boosted by the notoriety some of her guests had brought with them. The arrival of the stars of the traveling summer theatre festival had been like a free advertisement for the bed and breakfast. The Seaside Theatre Festival was a famous summer event that toured up and down the Atlantic coast each year, performing a new play in town theatres and even outdoor parks. It had been a major coup that the festival had not only picked Sweetfern Harbor as a stop on their tour this year, but even better – the Sheffield Bed and Breakfast would be where the actors would stay.

Word spread throughout Sweetfern Harbor like wildfire before their arrival. The well-known actress Ellen Teague was to feature as the star of the festival's play. Another big draw was the young and devastatingly handsome actor Shawn Quincy, who drew younger crowds that swooned like Elvis fans of an earlier era. There was also Anna Quincy, Shawn's young and talented wife, the acclaimed comedian Ricky Owens, and the young ingénue Bonnie Ross in her first role.

When Brenda received the phone call informing her about this prestigious booking, she had stood in shock looking at the list of names in her hand. Now that it was the day of their arrival, she found herself gazing at the list again.

"Are you nervous?" asked Allie. The sixteen-year-old beamed. Allie was her office manager when not in school. "I mean, it's really something that Ellen Teague will actually sleep in one of the beds upstairs." She breathed deeply and visibly swooned. "I have to say my favorite is that good-looking Shawn Quincy. Have you ever seen him dance? I'd love just one dance with him someday. I can only imagine his arms around me."

Brenda laughed fondly at the starstruck look in Allie's eyes. "Who knows? You may get your chance. Though I should remind you that he's married. I know Anna plays his wife in the show, too." Brenda paused and then answered Allie's question. "I guess I am a little nervous...but it's because I've always been a huge fan of Ellen Teague. I wonder what she's really like in person."

It was going to be a big weekend and everyone at Sheffield Bed and Breakfast scurried around to make things perfect. Brenda glanced through the wide sitting room window. In approximately one hour, the cast of the hit play "The Rich Game" would arrive.

As Brenda watched, Jenny Rivers parked in front, then jumped out to swing open the back door of her van. The florist unloaded an armful of beautiful floral arrangements.

"I have them all here, Brenda." Jenny elbowed the front door open and Brenda took the large vase from her, inhaling the sweet perfume of the arrangement. "I'll be bringing a lot more before this weekend is over. I'm already doing a booming business because of the theatre festival and your special guests."

"This is beautiful. I can always count on quality from you, Jenny. I'm glad this helps your business, too. Every shop on Main Street should have a good weekend."

"Are they here yet?" Jenny looked around the front hall of the bed and breakfast, her eyes wide with curiosity.

Brenda shook her head. "No, but they'll be here soon." Jenny's crestfallen face told her that the young florist, too, wanted to get a firsthand look at the prestigious guests. "Don't worry. You'll get to meet them all. Their first performance is tomorrow."

Jenny sighed. "I know, but I hoped I came at the right time

to see them check in. I have a few more vases in the car. Where do you want them?"

Brenda gave her instructions and Jenny offered to complete the arrangements by setting them up. Her talent was not just making beautiful bouquets, but choosing the perfect settings for them.

"If you want to, we can take the large spray of roses and dahlias up to Ellen Teague's quarters," Brenda offered. She delighted to see Jenny's reaction.

"I'd love to see where she is staying," said Jenny, fighting to refrain from gushing. She carried the large bouquet up to the suite reserved for the star. When Brenda unlocked the door, Jenny stepped inside and walked slowly around the spacious room that included a large walk-in closet with a dressing table.

"I gave her this room because the extra closet will hold all the costumes, and the dressing table is perfect for makeup. It was something she specifically asked for."

"Everything is just beautiful, Brenda." The florist gazed around the room, which had been polished and shined within an inch of its life.

Brenda was pleased that Jenny liked it so much. Allie had helped her brainstorm a few extra special finishing touches. The rich Belgian chocolates perched on the lace pillow sham and bottle of Moët and Chandon Champagne on the antique bureau with crystal champagne glasses would be enough to tempt anyone. She double-checked that the bathroom was impeccably clean and stocked with fresh, fluffy towels.

"Allie even had the idea to email Ellen's assistant and ask her what kinds of books she likes to read," said Brenda proudly, glancing at the small array of classics in several genres posed on the bedside console. A variety of movies had been added to the console as well, and an assortment of music, which included a couple of operas.

Jenny gazed around the room in awe at the attention to

detail. "I suppose you know Ellen Teague has won five Oscars and two Tony awards for her acting," said Brenda.

"And she's a famous director, too," added Jenny, adjusting the vase carefully where she had set it on an antique lace doily so it was reflected in the bureau mirror. Brenda nodded in admiration. There was little she did not know about Ellen Teague. Brenda found the woman fascinating. She lived a glamorous life that led Brenda's imagination in wild directions.

"Do you have time to show me where everyone else will stay?"

Brenda showed her the way to a smaller, tasteful room immediately next to Ellen's, which was to be for her personal assistant. "This room has access to Ellen's. It's for her assistant, Chester Boyd. I understand he makes all arrangements for her and is responsible for all the show's particulars. He also makes sure Ellen is comfortable and prepared."

They crossed the wide planked hallway to view the room where Shawn and Anna Quincy would stay and Jenny admired the stunning view of the cascading rose arbors in the garden below. After showing Jenny where everyone would be staying, Brenda turned to point out two doors at the far end of the hall.

"Those two are lucky, they are the only guests here who are not with the Seaside Theatre Festival. They are regulars here and come twice a year in the summer and in the winter. When I told them in confidence, they insisted they did not expect to get their usual quarters. I think they are thrilled to be here at the same time the performers are."

Just then, they heard voices downstairs and turned to look at each other in realization of who it must be. Brenda smiled at Jenny and said, "Here's your chance. If you want to see the cast firsthand, follow me." In her excitement, Jenny nearly tripped on the top step. Brenda reached out a hand to steady her and together they descended the staircase. As they reached the first floor, they heard the actors practically bubbling with excitement as they exclaimed over the beautiful décor of the Sheffield house. Brenda gestured for Jenny to wait to one side while she greeted her famous guests. It was going to be a perfect weekend at the bed and breakfast.

Brenda couldn't help but look behind everyone to search for her favorite star.

"If you are looking for Ellen, she is following us in her limousine. Chester is with her." Anna Quincy stepped toward Brenda and introduced herself. Brenda had seen Anna in a few movies and was not surprised to see that she was even more beautiful in person. Anna introduced her to everyone else, and Brenda tried to suppress the nervous flutter in her stomach as she shook the hands of these stars who had just stepped into her bed and breakfast.

When Brenda had everyone's attention, she gave them a warm welcome and passed out the room keys. The guests were shown to their rooms on the second floor, not far from the suite waiting for Ellen Teague.

"I hope everything meets your expectations," said Allie, hovering at Brenda's elbow as she watched Shawn open the door of the room for his young wife. Brenda pointed out Chester's and Ellen's rooms to Anna. "We felt this would serve their purposes, since he is her assistant. Also, there is plenty of room for costumes and makeup in her room."

"Are we the only ones booked this weekend?" asked Bonnie, who tucked one curling tress behind her ear as she stood in the doorway of her room.

"We have two other guests who always come this weekend every year, but they are separate from your group at the far end. You can see where the hallway turns a little. They are down there."

"This place must have a lot of nooks and crannies...or

maybe crooks and nannies," said Ricky, cracking a smile, "and plenty of stories to tell."

"It has a ton of history," Allie piped up eagerly, seeming to enjoy the moment when everyone's eyes landed on her. Brenda watched her young employee with amusement as she continued to tell them a portion of the old house's history with enthusiasm.

Before Allie could bore their guests, Brenda gently interrupted her to invite them all for refreshments. "The sitting room is just across from the front entrance. Our tea and pastries are famous, so I hope I'll see you downstairs."

When Brenda returned to the foyer, she found Jenny standing with her eyes wide and sparkling, watching as the entourage descended the stairs. As much as Jenny clearly wanted to linger, she excused herself with an excited smile at Brenda and then left to return to her shop.

In the sitting room, the housekeeper Phyllis Lindsey had laid a sumptuous spread of delicate pastries, fruit, and other treats, with a beautiful antique teapot and china teacups at the ready. The actors were charmed to meet the capable Phyllis and exclaimed at her excellent tea, and as they sat to eat their refreshments, the conversations were lively.

Bonnie Ross laughed easily and enjoyed everyone around her. Her curly auburn hair and warm demeanor seemed to spread a glow over every movement she made. When Brenda asked her role in the play, she smiled broadly.

"I'm rather new to this but have been cast in the role of the young hostess of the country estate where the play takes place. It's not a big part but it sure made me happy when I was cast for it. It's my first big break."

Brenda congratulated her. "My wife and I play the married couple," Shawn Quincy chimed in. "Do you know the play?" Brenda nodded, having read a brief description of "The Rich Game" in the local newspaper.

"And my role is the lowly husband of our luminous star,"

said Ricky Owens. The fortyish looking man tilted his head and humor was evident in his blue eyes. He stroked his beard as if by habit.

"I have heard of you," said Phyllis as she refilled Ricky's teacup. "You have won many awards."

"I'd say his biggest role is pretending to be Ellen's husband," said Shawn with dry humor. "I'm sure you have to agree with that, Ricky."

Ricky rolled his eyes. "I've managed."

Brenda picked up a vibe she couldn't put her finger on. The actors seemed at ease with one another, but they conveyed something more without words. Before she could ask a question, Allie jumped up at the sound of a limousine pulling up in front of the bed and breakfast. All eyes turned to look at the open doorway that led to the check-in counter. No one spoke and Brenda leapt to her feet with excitement.

But when she reached the foyer, her enthusiastic welcome for Ellen Teague faded a little when she saw that the much-admired star stood coldly before her and barely returned her greeting. Her idol stood before her in a pale green silk dress, tasteful heels, and a wide-brimmed hat. It was a strange contrast to the amiable and relaxed scene she had just exited.

A man stepped toward Brenda and extended his hand. "I am Chester Boyd, and this is Miss Teague," he said, shaking her hand formally.

Brenda had been expecting a young assistant, but Chester reminded her more of a butler. His perfectly coiffed dark hair held tinges of grey. His stance was erect and his attention was focused entirely on Ellen Teague.

"I presume Miss Teague's quarters are ready for her?" His arched eyebrows indicated a demand rather than a question.

"Of course, please follow me."

When Brenda turned to lead them upstairs, she caught a glimpse of the coal black hair and pale skin of Ellen Teague. She knew the woman was younger than her own forty-six years, but right now the star looked ten years older than Brenda. And that famous face she had seen so many times on the screen looked different. Under the brim of her hat, her dark eyes were outlined with heavy makeup.

Ellen surveyed the foyer from top to bottom, prompting Brenda to wait at the foot of the stairs. So far, her idol had not spoken. Brenda tried to chalk the aloof manner up to the tiresome drive to Sweetfern Harbor, even though it wasn't that far from New York City. Brenda waited for the next move.

At last, Ellen Teague turned toward the staircase, and Chester followed close behind her. When she opened the door, Brenda held her breath while the actress walked slowly around the suite. In the sunlight that fell through the lace curtains, a sapphire ring gleamed on Ellen's slender finger and caught Brenda's eye. She noted that it matched her earrings and necklace. The silk dress Ellen wore was from Versace. Brenda recognized the design instantly since she had dreamed about owning one just like it ever since seeing it on the cover of Vogue magazine. Ellen lifted the large-brimmed hat from her head and Chester stepped forward in time to take it from her. At last, she spoke.

"Every costume must be dry-cleaned and pressed before our opening night tomorrow. I take it that is one of your duties?"

"I have someone who can take care of that right away for you, I know the owner of the dry-cleaner here in town. I am the owner of the bed and breakfast and I have very capable staff who will take care of that for you."

Ellen sniffed and her eyes ran over Brenda as if assessing her dress code as owner of the establishment. "That will be all."

Chester followed Brenda into the hallway. "You will have to excuse Miss Teague. She has had a trying last few days rehearsing and preparing for the performances this weekend."

Brenda smiled and assured him she understood. As she walked back downstairs, she tried to imagine the glitz and glamor of the life of a star – but also the work and the demanding schedule. She hoped the arrogant attitude Ellen displayed was indeed due to stress and fatigue, and was not her usual demeanor. Every time she had seen her in movies, Brenda had come away with an impression of her as a strong but ultimately warm woman, someone with tremendous depth and feeling. Surely it was not all an act.

When she entered the sitting room, the atmosphere was noticeably subdued. Anna whispered something to her husband and Shawn nodded in agreement. Even Ricky Owens appeared lost in his thoughts as he gazed out the window, his eyes fixated on the side lawn and gardens of Sheffield Bed and Breakfast. Brenda glanced at young Bonnie Ross and caught her eye with a questioning glance. Bonnie answered her with only a lopsided grin and then excused herself from the room.

Allie saved the day when she bounded into the room to offer a tour of the grounds. Her sudden interruption was like a breath of fresh air in the room, and the actors happily followed her outside, more than ready to take in the salt breeze and the lush gardens and leave the strange hush of the sitting room behind.

chapter two

Brenda headed up to her apartment for a much-needed break after getting her guests settled in. Halfway up the stairs, she greeted Chester on his way down. He bowed slightly and stopped at the landing where a stained-glass window filtered prettily colored light onto a velvet-cushioned window seat.

"I looked at the books in Miss Teague's room. Are they first editions as requested?"

"I am not sure. A few may be." In fact, Brenda had not thought to ask Allie if there had been such specific instructions in the email.

"Please check, since I was quite specific. Miss Teague refuses to read anything except first editions."

Brenda stared at him. Chester returned her look wordlessly. He then turned and walked back up the stairs just as his boss called his name. Evidently, Ellen Teague demanded his services. Brenda hoped Ellen would get a good night's sleep so as to awaken in a better mood the next day. Without even going to her apartment, she turned to go back downstairs and down the narrow passageway to the kitchen. She was determined to make sure that the dinner menu was scrutinized and every detail perfected. Together with the chef, she carefully reviewed the menu and they discussed every request from Ellen, who had sent additional requests regarding the evening meal.

"Add more variety to the side dishes with the entrée in case the others don't like what she has ordered for the table," Brenda said, fretting as she surveyed everything in preparation stages laid out in the kitchen.

"I will do everything to keep all guests satisfied during the evening meal, Brenda." Her chef, Morgan, a talented woman in her mid-fifties, was always her rock in the storm, and had weathered Brenda's nerves many times. She gave her boss a patient smile.

Brenda patted Morgan's arm in thanks and reminded herself that her chef's culinary skills were renowned for a reason. Allie was next on her list. She found her trooping back into the house through the rear hallway with the cast members, who thanked the young girl and headed up to their rooms. Brenda told Allie of Chester's inquiry regarding the first editions.

"Is there a difference? I got her a bunch of beautiful copies of classics, like her assistant said."

"No, first editions are when a book was printed for the first time. The classics especially are in high demand if they are first editions – they can fetch thousands of dollars and be collector's items." Brenda shook her head. "Apparently, she likes her new books to be first editions, too. She is a particular woman, it seems. Will you please look in our library and try to find some first editions? I know my uncle had a number of them in there."

"I'll look for some. How do I know if they are the right ones?"

"They'll only have one year listed on the publication page. Find whatever you can and I'll run the titles past Chester." Brenda sighed as they walked to the library. Her perfect weekend was off to a rocky start.

Allie hesitated with her hand on the doorknob of the library. "The rest of the cast kept making remarks about her. I don't think they like her much."

"It may prove to be a long weekend," said Brenda, "but we'll get through it. Let's just try to keep this kind of gossip under wraps – I would be mortified if she found out the staff was talking about her like this." Allie nodded somberly and Brenda hoped her young employee would take the admonishment to heart. She changed the topic. "You know, I'm really looking forward to seeing 'The Rich Game.' I hear it got rave reviews in New York."

The teenager stepped into the library and gazed out the window, which looked out across the lawn to the street. Suddenly her eyes lit up. "Never mind the play...don't you have a date tonight with Mac?"

Brenda caught her breath and followed Allie's glance to see a familiar car pull up to the curb. "I had no idea it was this late. We're supposed to go down to the Italian café that just opened on Main Street." Allie grinned at her.

Brenda hurried to a small mahogany-framed mirror that hung on the wall of the library and smoothed down her hair, feeling a fluttering sensation like a butterfly in her stomach.

The door to the foyer opened and she stepped into the hall to greet the handsome Detective Mac Rivers. He gave Brenda a warm, meaningful look that made her heart skip a beat. He bent and kissed her lightly.

"I suppose your celebrities made it in okay." The masculine timbre of his voice suddenly reminded her that a date was more interesting than dealing with Ellen Teague.

Brenda glanced at her watch impatiently. "They'll be down for dinner in a few minutes. I'll just welcome them to the table and then I'll freshen up and be ready in no time. I'm excited to try out that new café."

She had already asked Allie and Phyllis to take charge of

serving dinner. Brenda crossed her fingers hoping there wouldn't be any glitches, but she knew she was lucky to have such a responsible and reliable staff to step in for her.

Brenda changed for her date and came back down to greet Mac again. "I'm so glad to see you, but I don't want to take longer than an hour and a half away, especially tonight," said Brenda, glancing worriedly toward the closed door of the dining room.

"You seem a little nervous. Is it because your favorite star Ellen Teague is here?" he teased.

"She's actually rather demanding and I'm worried that we got off to a bad start. But I trust Allie and Phyllis. And you know, Phyllis has an uncanny sense of intuition for certain things." She laughed. "I think she will foresee any demands Ellen will have before they come to a head."

"Then let's go and try out that Italian food." His eyes lit up with a special warmth and Brenda wondered what he was planning. "I have something special for you tonight after dinner." When they got to his car, he reached inside and handed her a bouquet of wildflowers. "These are for you, but they are only a teaser. Jenny told me you always love the wildflowers when they arrive at her shop." Brenda took the gorgeous bouquet and smelled the delicate blooms, which looked like they had been plucked from a mountain meadow.

"Your daughter knows me well. They are beautiful. Thank you." She looked from her flowers up to the night sky and felt the gentle evening breeze on her skin. "Let's leave the bouquet in the car until after dinner and walk down to the café."

"I like that idea." He took her arm and his closeness sent shivers down her spine as they walked together into town.

She admired the detective in many ways. Not only was he good at his job but he was the perfect gentleman when it came to courting a woman. She couldn't help but feel safe and cherished and ladylike when he was around, and it was a pleasure to go for a simple walk down the sidewalk on the arm of such a handsome man.

They came to the café with its intimate lighting and cozy tables and Brenda thought she had never seen something so enticing in her life. Mac pulled out her chair when they approached a corner table. Their server lit the candle in the center and handed them menus. Aromas drifted into the dining room every time a server came and went from the kitchen. The night promised to be a perfect one, except Brenda couldn't get Ellen off her mind.

Mac could tell she was still troubled, and so he asked her more about what happened. She attempted to describe the star to Mac. She told him of her rudeness and repeated the story about the first editions.

"Maybe she gets like that before a performance. I've heard it's common for show people to be on edge before a big performance night," said Mac. "It could be her mental status is on the brink hoping things go as well as they did in New York. The town is overflowing with tourists who are here mainly to see her perform." Mac smiled at her. "Just give her a chance. I'm sure things will be a whole lot different tomorrow."

His logic made sense to her and Brenda realized she had overreacted. "I'm sure you're right. I've always admired her and have seen every movie she ever made – I shouldn't have placed such high expectations on her, perhaps."

When the Caesar salads arrived at their table, Mac told her a funny story of something that happened with his boss at work. Police Chief Bob Ingram was a serious man and plain spoken. The story revolved around a long spiel the chief gave a prisoner's wife about the necessity of searching her before the visit. He turned her over to an officer nearby and then was flabbergasted when the officer struggled to keep a smile off her face. Then the young officer explained the woman didn't know a word of English.

The story was humorous and Mac was a great storyteller but Brenda knew she laughed harder than it deserved. The relief she felt at not being near Ellen Teague right now was something that surprised her. Mac had assessed it all correctly and she hoped she managed to shake the star from her mind for the rest of the evening. Ellen Teague simply needed a good night's sleep. And Brenda Sheffield needed a good night out.

"Now that you've loosened up, let's finish this meal and get some fresh air." He picked up his fork. "I've been waiting for months to try this place out. Did I tell you I lived in Italy for a year? It was back in college, but I've never forgotten how much I liked their food."

"I still have a lot to learn about you, Mac Rivers." Brenda smiled to herself, picturing a young Mac strolling through the streets of an Italian village. She dug into her linguine in clam sauce with gusto and he did the same with his fettuccine alfredo.

As they finished dinner, Brenda's curiosity about his surprise returned. "Mac, I'm too curious...let's skip dessert," she said. Mac chuckled. In the glimmer of the candlelit restaurant, the combination of his blonde hair and startling blue eyes gave him a boyish look. He was a few years younger than she was, but the slight age difference didn't deter the mutual attraction that was like an electrified connection between them.

One thing he loved about Brenda was her insatiable curiosity. She was like a child waiting for Christmas morning. He loved indulging her, so he declined dessert as well and paid the bill.

Once outside, he drew her away from the wide windows

of the café toward the wide sweep of the Atlantic Ocean and took her gently into his arms as they watched the glimmer of the moon on the water. Then he stepped back and pulled a tiny velveteen box from his pocket. Her eyes opened wide as she turned to watch him.

"Brenda, since the day you arrived here I have loved you." He opened the box and she saw a delicate, sparkling ring. On closer observation, it didn't look like an engagement ring. She wasn't quite ready for a step like that anyway, and waited with bated breath for his next words. "This is not an engagement ring. At least, not yet. This is my promise of love for you. I want to develop a deeper love and friendship and learn all I can about you. This is a promise ring for you that hopefully will bring us together, even closer than we are now. I hope you will accept it in the same spirit I offer it to you."

Her relief spilled out. "I love the idea of a promise ring. It is a step forward for us. Thank you, Mac. I accept." She stepped closer to him, looking deeply in his eyes, and he reached out to take her hand in his.

He slipped the ring onto her finger. His arms enfolded her again and he drew her close. People coming and going from the restaurant looked their way and smiled. Brenda released a happy sigh and stepped back from the embrace to smile back. Then she turned to Mac, realizing what came next. There was a catch in her voice she tried to control. "We'd better get moving," she said.

"I don't want our night to be over so soon, but you're right. It's a big weekend for you."

They walked back to Sheffield Bed and Breakfast, her arm tucked under his. Brenda felt the promise ring gleaming on her finger with happiness and hope, but she turned her mind resolutely toward her duties. When they reached the Sheffield, lights blazed from nearly every room, spilling out across the lawn in the darkness. Brenda silently thanked her

Uncle Randolph Sheffield for leaving the Queen Anne-style mansion establishment to her. She had met him only once as a very young child but had never forgotten his kindness to her. In memory of that kindness, she vowed that she would not be deterred by her guest's cold demeanor.

"It looks like everything is still standing" she said, realizing she was stalling. She gazed at the wide front porch that wrapped around the house to one side where several sturdy antique rocking chairs sat vacant. "Oh, let's not go inside yet." She led him around to the privacy of the backyard where the rose arbors trailed down the garden's edge and the view of the sea. They sat down in the Adirondack chairs and listened to the waves that lapped against the rocks. Far in the distance they could see the lights of a large ship far out at sea. "I once thought of replacing the paintings throughout the bed and breakfast. Did you know that?"

"I didn't know that, but I'm glad you didn't. Randolph was very proud of his collection of nautical paintings. Those old ships are stunning."

Brenda laughed softly. "I've gotten used to them. Though sometimes, on a night like tonight, it makes me wish I could jump into one of those old paintings and sail away to sea. Just like in the old days."

Mac reached for her hand and clasped it in his. They sat in silence. Breathing in the salt air enhanced their senses. Every smell and sound under the star-studded night sky held them both spellbound. Brenda wordlessly said a prayer of thanks for her wonderful life and for the man sitting next to her.

"I hate to give this up, but I should get back inside and check on things. The cast will be out most of tomorrow for rehearsals before the first performance tomorrow night."

"I'll pick you up early enough for the play. I hope I'm not too late to get tickets. I hear they are selling out fast."

"I didn't realize you hadn't gotten the tickets yet. If they are sold out we can go the second night."

She tried to hide her disappointment. She knew Mac was busy at the police station and she had not thought about tickets. Preparing her staff and the bed and breakfast for the guests had consumed her energies.

"I'll make it work somehow, Brenda. I just let that slip up on me. I'm sorry."

"Don't worry about it. We'll see it soon enough. If we miss getting tickets for the first performance I'm sure there are tickets for the second one still available. If we miss tomorrow night it will give us more time together, just the two of us."

Mac's mouth curved in a slow smile. "I like that idea."

After retrieving her flowers from Mac's car and kissing him goodnight, she went into the bed and breakfast. Allie met her at the door and gushed about the dinner, which had been praised as delicious by all the actors – except Ellen.

"Ellen ate very little and left the table midway through the meal. We couldn't tell if it was the food or if she just wasn't hungry." Brenda caught her breath to hear this. "Really, things went fine, Brenda," Allie reassured her. She followed Brenda to the kitchen where she retrieved a vase for her flowers. "And Chester followed her upstairs. Everyone else stayed and enjoyed the food and drinks later. Shawn told us not to worry, Ellen does that often."

"Did she complain about the food?"

Allie shook her head. "Nope. She just left and Chester followed her. Phyllis went up later and asked her if she wanted a hot dinner or dessert or a snack brought up to her room. Ellen declined but Phyllis thought Chester might want to eat something. So she left a covered hot dinner outside his room. She put it in a warmer so it would stay hot." Brenda was gratified to hear that Phyllis's gift of intuition had once again provided a special touch for their guests.

"Perhaps Ellen will be in a better mood tomorrow after she's had a good night's sleep," Brenda commented.

"I'm not so sure about that. Even Ricky Owens made a

snide remark about her after she left, and he wasn't joking this time."

"Allie, remember these are our guests. My uncle would have said they deserve kind treatment no matter what we may overhear, remember that. Let's just see what tomorrow brings. Thank you for doing a good job tonight. I'll go see Phyllis now. Goodnight."

When she knocked on Phyllis's door, the fiftyish woman opened it with a smile. When Brenda walked in, she saw William Pendleton sitting in an armchair with a glass of wine in his hand.

"I'm sorry. I didn't realize you were here, William." She turned to Phyllis. "I'll see you in the morning before breakfast. I mainly wanted to thank you for taking over tonight. Allie told me of your thoughtfulness toward Chester. I'm sure he was quite hungry for something."

William waved his hand. "There's no need for an apology. I'll be leaving now."

"You stay right where you are, William," said Phyllis. "There are no secrets between us and unless Brenda is reluctant to speak in front of you it is fine that you listen in." Phyllis looked at Brenda questioningly.

"I have no problem if he hears. I just wanted to ask if you knew why Ellen didn't stay for dinner." Brenda inquired about the menu and the email with its many requests, hoping there had not been some detail amiss.

Phyllis spread her hands open. "She just up and left without saying anything really. Chester followed her out and no one said anything until they were out of earshot. Several people made cutting remarks about it but no one dwelled on the matter. It helped when she left since everyone loosened up and enjoyed the meal."

"I think the weight of her responsibilities is taking its toll on her. After all, it's just before an important performance and a lot depends on her."

"It is Ellen's way," said William. "She can be uptight at times." He laughed as the two women swiveled to look at him in surprised curiosity. "Yes, I know her somewhat. I had a hand in persuading the theatre festival to come here."

They chatted briefly about Ellen as William explained how they had met at a long-ago party when Ellen had been just a young Broadway star and William had worked in New York City. Over the years they had met many times, and he had followed her career avidly, even donating to support the Seaside Theatre Festival. Despite her curiosity, Brenda could tell the couple were eager to get back to their glasses of wine, and she soon bid them goodnight.

On her way to her apartment on the second floor, she took a side stairway, hoping not to run into anyone. She thought about how William and Phyllis had found true love later in life. They were compatible and she was sure they would tie the knot soon. William Pendleton was a very wealthy man, having inherited the vast holdings his wife had hoarded before her untimely death. He was kind and devoted to every person in the tight-knit seaside town of Sweetfern Harbor. She felt sure Phyllis would leave Sheffield Bed and Breakfast once she married William, despite her housekeeper's dedication to the bed and breakfast and indebtedness to Brenda's late Uncle Randolph Sheffield. Whether Phyllis stayed or departed, Brenda found herself smiling at the thought of her as William's future wife.

As she approached her apartment door, Brenda turned when she heard Chester Boyd's voice.

"Ms. Sheffield. I meant to deliver these to you earlier but your housekeeper told me you were out for a while." He handed her two tickets to the first performance of the play.

But before Brenda could reply, she heard Ellen Teague call to him from her room, in an imperious voice. He nodded in response to Brenda's hurried thanks as he turned on his heel to go.

Brenda felt overjoyed at this stroke of luck and felt that perhaps Uncle Randolph was watching over her. She quickly opened the door to her suite of rooms and called Mac to give him the good news.

chapter three

Early the next morning, Chester approached Brenda
again just as she was entering the dining room for
breakfast.

"Miss Teague has requested to use the back lawn for the
final rehearsal. I hope this is not a great inconvenience for
you."

Brenda froze in the doorway and took in the cool look in
Chester's eyes. She had not expected this but was determined
to make the best of it for her famous guests. "Of course, we
would be happy to have it here. What time will she expect
things to be ready?"

"The cast will be in costume by ten this morning. She does
not want this advertised, so please advise your staff to be
discreet. There will be no 'fans' admitted to the rehearsal." He
gave this last command with an air of disapproval and
finality, glancing at Allie as she walked past them into the
dining room. "But if the staff is free, they are welcome to
watch," he finished.

Brenda was both pleasantly surprised at this offer and
anxious to know what arrangements would need to be made
for scenery or props. Chester waved her concerns aside. "You
do not have to worry about any of that. The particulars have

been arranged. The costumes are back from the dry-cleaners and everything is ready."

Brenda thanked Chester and as she ate a hasty breakfast, made a mental note to give her staff a bonus when the weekend was over and the cast had departed from the bed and breakfast. This was turning into a much different weekend than she had at first envisioned. Ten minutes later, she gathered everyone in the kitchen with the chef to tell them of the developments. Although Morgan was already busy with preparations for dinner, Brenda asked her to make fresh lemonade to be served on the lawn as refreshments for the actors. Allie offered to step in to bake cookies and Phyllis offered to make a tray of sandwiches to be set out, and the chef nodded her thanks to both of them.

Since there were still a couple hours before the rehearsal was due to begin, Brenda directed Phyllis to first clean any of the vacated rooms to get a head start. "Anyone who has gone to put on their costume and get into makeup – start with their rooms. Leave Ellen's suite until the rehearsal begins. In between times you can help down here with the food. Thank you, all of you. Please remember we have been invited to watch the rehearsal but we must be discreet. Ellen doesn't want word to get around town and I'd hate to see the look on Chester's face if some tourists appeared in the garden. If we can, let's watch out for any stragglers and try to redirect them before they try walking around to the back garden today, okay?"

Brenda planned to supervise and especially ensure no unwanted guests wandered through the rehearsal, but secretly she was thrilled to be immersed in the theatre world. Her interest in Hollywood, Broadway and all things show business peaked now that it was literally at her doorstep. She stood on the lawn and watched as the final preparations were made. The cast members, transformed into their characters with the aid of sumptuous costumes and expert stage makeup, stood waiting for Ellen Teague. Though she was the star, she was also the director.

When Ellen finally appeared on the lawn and called out, "Places!" to her fellow actors to start the show, Brenda could practically see the tension in the air. For it seemed that Ellen Teague's mood had not improved overnight. The bright sunny day with soft ocean breezes didn't improve it, either. Brenda held her breath watching the star command the other actors with only a few subtle words, or an imperious shake of her head. She demanded perfection, and as the rehearsal wore on, she had the actors run through certain scenes over and over again as she focused on errors that Brenda could not even discern from the audience. Even though it was supposed to be a comedy, the smallest infraction was elevated to something that would either make or break the entire performance according to Ellen.

After two hours of rehearsal, the sun was high in the sky when Allie rolled a large cart onto the lawn with platters of sandwiches, lemonade and iced tea. Ellen broke her focus from the scene to glance at the long table and announced a break.

Brenda was relieved on behalf of the actors, several of whom seemed to be sweating slightly in their costumes. She went to the end of the table to help Allie arrange the cookies on a large platter and to pour drinks for the weary actors.

If Brenda had been hoping to talk to her idol over lunch, she had to quickly swallow her disappointment. She watched out of the corner of her eye as Ellen spoke briefly to Chester, then went to sit some distance away at a small table under an elm tree. Chester filled a plate for her and carried it over to her, returning for his own plate and their drinks. Brenda resolved to not let Ellen spoil her day, so when she sat down with her own sandwich, she started a conversation with Anna Quincy.

"I loved you in that scene just now. How long have you been an actress?"

"Not long, actually. I have been a ballet dancer since I was quite young – that's how I met Shawn. He was older than I but every time his class got a break, he used to watch my classes through the studio windows." She smiled at the memory. "He later went on to Broadway and performed in many shows as a dancer, and then started auditioning for acting roles as well. On Broadway, if you're a dancer you practically have to be an actor, too! By that time, I became an understudy for the same shows."

"How did you get this role?"

Shawn joined his wife, setting down a cup of iced tea before her. "Don't let her fool you...there are a couple of minor dance scenes in 'The Rich Game,' but we both auditioned for this one because we wanted speaking roles for a change. We think it is rejuvenating to try something different once in a while. This is Anna's first big role." Adoration filled his eyes as he gazed at his beautiful young wife.

Ricky Owens joined them. Brenda was getting a feel for how the actors all seemed to be so friendly with each other that they naturally gravitated to each other for conversation – all except Ellen, of course. She had to laugh at her train of thought because at that very moment, young Bonnie walked up balancing her plate and drink and pouted prettily at the lack of chairs to join them, and someone immediately suggested they all move to the longer picnic table set up on the small flagstone patio on one side of the garden. With a dimpled grin, Bonnie insisted that Brenda join them. Brenda happily grabbed her sandwich and drink and followed the cast.

"Sheffield Bed and Breakfast is just wonderful. Like a place from another time. It's strange though not to see Randolph around. We all miss him," said Ricky. Brenda turned to regard him with surprise. "If you ever wanted to watch a real actor it would have been Randolph Sheffield."

"That's to say nothing of his directing talent," said Anna.

Brenda was speechless. The others chimed in and couldn't say enough about their time working with her uncle on stage.

"I never knew he was in show business," she said. Then it was their turn to stare at her in amazement.

"He was so talented," said Ricky. "How did you not know this about him?"

"I guess I'm wondering that myself, too. I didn't know him well at all. My parents spoke of him on occasion but I never once heard them say anything about a career in show business. We lived in Michigan and only visited once when I was a young child. And I knew that later he retired and turned the house into a bed and breakfast, but I guess I never knew what he had retired from."

"Anna and I worked with him often but didn't know him as well as Ricky and Ellen did. He wasn't just good on stage – he was always so generous and kind to everyone," said Shawn. "Wasn't Chester a good friend of his, too, before he started working for Ellen?" He turned to Ricky for verification.

"Yes, they were very good friends. Chester was a great admirer of Randolph's, too. As I recall, Randolph had already inherited a fortune when he was young – he decided to get into acting and directing because it was his passion, not because it made him a star. Anyway, I'm surprised no one mentioned this before. We loved Randolph so much, that's why we just had to come to Sweetfern Harbor for the touring theatre festival and stay in the bed and breakfast that was his home and business for so many years. I think he is the one who convinced the Seaside Theatre Festival to come here in the first place."

Bonnie seemed to take in Brenda's pensive look and laid a gentle hand on her arm. "Although I never met your uncle, I have heard a lot about him. He was a role model for many young actors like me. I hope to give back to the community one day as generously as he did."

Brenda was lost in thought as the conversation moved on around her. She decided she must explore the attic of the bed and breakfast at the first opportunity. She knew much of her uncle's things had been stored in crates there after his death. She had a lot to learn about him. Her thoughts were interrupted when Ellen Teague's voice cut through the chatter.

"I too knew Randolph well," Ellen said, approaching their table. "We were a well-known pair in the early days. We could have enjoyed our fame together if he hadn't decided to suddenly move down to this godforsaken hamlet." She looked around the lawn disparagingly and then turned to Brenda. "We'll have to talk about that later. We must continue with the rehearsal now."

Brenda nodded. She shivered at the tone of voice Ellen had used. The others did not comment on her cold remark and Ellen whisked them back to rehearsal. After the happy spell of the conversation around her had been broken by Ellen, watching the rehearsal seemed to have lost some of its former glamor. She felt the need to be alone. She made sure that her chef Morgan remembered that dinner would be an hour early, to give the cast time to leave for the outdoor theatre at Harbor Park, then climbed the stairs to her rooms.

Once in her apartment, Brenda poured a glass of iced tea and settled back in her easy chair. When this weekend was over, she planned to spend a lot of time in the attic opening crates that held her uncle's past life. It would be an excellent way to relax after Ellen Teague's stressful presence at the bed and breakfast.

That evening, her cell phone rang. Mac told her he would be there in forty-five minutes to pick her up for the performance. The call ended and Brenda quickly showered and got ready. She had read reviews again for the comedy and couldn't wait to see it. She hoped to regain her admiration for Ellen Teague by becoming immersed in the play and forgetting about everything else that had happened. In no time at all, she heard Mac's unmistakable voice filter up the stairs from the front desk. The bed and breakfast had been quiet since the actors had left for Harbor Park. Brenda smiled in anticipation of a wonderful night and picked up the tickets from her bureau and hurried down to meet Mac.

As he took her arm and they walked toward the park, she noticed him glance down at her hand to peek at the delicate promise ring on her finger. "Did you know this play is a comedy of sorts?"

"I know all about it," said Brenda. "I got to see some of the rehearsal. The play takes place at a country estate and then the two main couples switch partners as an experiment. It's sort of like Wife Swap, the reality TV show. I think it's interesting that Ellen gets paired with Shawn. I wonder how she decided that."

"She probably decided since he was so good-looking she had to be paired with him." Mac winked at her. "That's why you agreed to date me, isn't it?"

She jabbed his arm and teased back. As they entered the park, they saw most of the population of Sweetfern Harbor, not to mention a large number of tourists, and they quickly found their seats amid the crowd. One empty seat was next to Brenda and she wondered who would be sitting there. It didn't take long to find out. Edward Graham, her lawyer and a fixture in Sweetfern Harbor, arrived and greeted them warmly.

As they chatted with Edward, Brenda saw that William Pendleton and Phyllis Lindsey were seated only a few rows ahead. Their heads together, they whispered back and forth to one another. Brenda smiled to hear Phyllis's soft laugh. Directly behind them sat Phyllis's daughter Molly, who owned the popular Morning Sun Coffee shop on Main Street, and her boyfriend Pete Graham, the postman who delivered mail around Sweetfern Harbor, including to Sheffield Bed and Breakfast. As they waited for the lights to dim, the conversation between old and new friends was lively. Brenda leaned over to greet Mac's daughter Jenny and her friend Hope, who owned the bakery that supplied pastries to the bed and breakfast. The air of anticipation finally broke when the lights dimmed and all eyes focused on the outdoor stage.

Edward leaned close to Brenda and whispered. "I have some news for you, Brenda. Will you have some time right after the performance to talk?"

She looked at his face. Whatever he had to say must be serious stuff. "I'll see you then," she whispered back. Brenda watched the story unfolding on stage and was soon taken in by Ellen's skills and by the comedic talents of the entire cast. It was easy to forget Ellen's offstage personality as she transformed into a witty and glamorous wife whose ribald lines with Shawn's character had the audience holding their sides with laughter. Anna and Ricky, whose characters had been paired off unhappily in the other wife swap, engineered a hilarious prank in revenge, and the ingénue Bonnie appeared at the end as the young country heiress who saved the day and righted all wrongs. When the lights came down, the audience immediately jumped to their feet in a standing ovation. After three encores and a multitude of bouquets were handed to the actors and actresses, it was agreed by all that "The Rich Game" measured up to everyone's expectations.

"I plan to come back tomorrow if I can get a ticket," said Jenny with enthusiasm. "This is the best show I've seen in a long time."

Everyone around her agreed and immediately began making plans to come back, but Brenda realized this might be her chance to get to the attic sooner rather than later. She set aside her initial idea to wait until the weekend was over. Seeing such a wonderful play made her determined to delve into her uncle's life right away.

As the crowds thinned, Brenda told Mac to wait a few minutes. "Edward wants to tell me something. I think it must be important since he wanted to talk right after the show."

"Don't worry about me. I'll sit over there on that bench and wait."

Edward suggested they walk a few yards away from everyone. "Ellen Teague met with me earlier today." His eyes avoided hers. "There is a court case involving you and your uncle's estate. She tells me you do not own Sheffield Bed and Breakfast. I don't have all the details yet but it is first on my agenda tomorrow. I won't wait for Monday to find out whether her claims have merit."

Brenda closed her mouth when she realized it was wide open with shock. "But...I was named in his will. He owned the bed and breakfast and he left it to me. That's all there is to it. The will is a legal document. You were his lawyer, Edward, so you should know."

"Simmer down. I told you I still have to get the details, though I doubt she is telling the whole truth of the matter. Still, I will look into it and let you know whatever I find out."

When she returned to Mac she had a heavy heart. Her eyes fell on the cast members who were just then leaving the stage area. A group of fans, journalists, and reporters swarmed toward them, and Ellen Teague stepped forward to claim the center of attention. Even from a distance Brenda could see a few of the actors exchange glances and roll their eyes as Ellen flashed a brilliant smile for the cameras. There was no doubt that Ellen's fame and attitude caused a great deal of tension and Brenda felt sorry for the other actors. They all did a fantastic job on stage. Brenda waited a few moments, watching the hubbub across the park's lawn from where she stood.

Mac didn't ask questions but knew that something was definitely wrong. Whatever it was that Edward Graham had to discuss, it apparently wasn't good news. They watched the actors pose under the starry summer sky for a photo – Ellen posing glamorously in front and the rest of the cast arrayed behind her. When Mac turned to look at Brenda again, for a moment he thought she was about to cry. Then he looked closer and saw that her cheeks were flushed as if with righteous anger.

"Let's go home, Brenda. You look like you need a breather."

Brenda took one more look at the actors, then turned to nod at Mac. She wanted nothing more than to confront Ellen head-on and find out what this lawsuit was all about.

She allowed Mac to steer her homeward. "I don't want the news getting out but Edward just told me the Sheffield Bed and Breakfast may not belong to me." As Mac turned to look at her in surprise, she told Mac about the blow Edward's news had dealt her.

"He will get to the bottom of this," said Mac. "He filed the will and you signed the papers, I can't imagine what could change that. Let's stop and get a drink to end the night."

They stopped at a small bar and grill at the end of Main Street and sat listening to the live music played by a small acoustic band on the deck that looked out toward the street. She sipped a glass of red wine while he enjoyed a cold beer and they watched the crowds from the theatre festival trickling home down Main Street. It was a beautiful night and she should have been relaxing with the man she loved, but her mind was racing. Brenda finally stifled a yawn and told him she was beat. "I'll talk to you tomorrow. Edward is going to look things over in the morning rather than wait until

Monday so I'll call you when I hear something." Mac, still worried about her, walked her home with a protective arm wrapped around her shoulders.

At the door to the bed and breakfast, Mac leaned down. His kiss lingered longer than usual. She smiled up at him, the warm glow of his embrace permeating her body, and turned to go inside. He waved over his shoulder as he walked back down the street, knowing Brenda would be looking at him from the front windows as she always did. She climbed the stairs wearily to her apartment hoping that Edward would soon have good news for her.

chapter four

The Blossoms van pulled up in front of Sheffield Bed and Breakfast the next morning. Allie peeked out the front door and saw Jenny Rivers unloading spray after spray of beautiful bouquets, many of them roses. She went outside to lend a hand.

"Good morning, Jenny. Did Brenda order all these flowers?"

"Not all of them. Most are deliveries for Ellen Teague. There are more of them coming, I'll have to make a second delivery run later today. I'm just hoping I don't run out. If I do, I'll have to get the florist in the next town over to help me out."

Brenda appeared in the doorway just as Allie and Jenny carried up several armfuls to the front porch. Allie told her most of the flowers were for the famous star.

"I separated yours from Ellen's," said Jenny. She pointed to the cluster set aside on the porch. "As soon as I get them all inside you can tell me where you want them. I have the newspaper with early morning reviews with me, too, if you want an extra copy." Her eyes sparkled. Sweetfern Harbor's visiting star certainly increased business in the village. The whole town had come alive.

"Let's take as many as we can carry up to her room," said Brenda. She solicited Allie's help and the three made their way upstairs.

Brenda knocked on the door. When it opened, she saw Ellen Teague perfectly coiffed and with makeup on, but she was more astonished by the exquisite silk dressing gown she wore. The emerald green silk contrasted with her dark eyes that glittered in the morning sunshine. Brenda did not know if she would get used to this kind of glamor in her bed and breakfast.

Ellen did not appear surprised at the numerous bouquets and immediately directed them where to place each bouquet. The lavish floral displays spilled their incredible perfumes into the room and looked magnificent when set up on the bureau and the dressing table.

"There are more to come," said Jenny. "We'll bring them up right away."

Ellen had no comment and turned back to the mirror where she patted her hair in place. Allie and Jenny started for the door when Ellen decided to speak.

"Bring just a few more up here. The rest can be displayed prominently throughout the bed and breakfast."

Jenny and Allie glanced at Brenda. Her look told them to quickly go and get the rest. As for Brenda, she tried to take a calming breath. Ellen had made a generous offer, but it wasn't the actress's prerogative to command her to place them prominently – but Brenda ignored that for the moment. Brenda took a deep breath and got right to the issue.

"What is this about a court case against my Uncle Randolph's estate challenging me as the rightful owner of the bed and breakfast?"

Ellen turned to look at her briefly, then rolled her eyes dismissively as she stood up to face her. "Oh, you silly girl, you do not own this place. I'm the one with a stronger legal claim to it." She advanced toward Brenda as she said this, and Brenda instinctively took a step back toward the door. "It will all be sorted out soon. This place needs a lot of improvements but I'll manage that. Not that I plan to spend much time here but it is mine nevertheless." Without waiting for a response, she gently pushed Brenda through the doorway with one manicured hand and closed the door in her face.

"You can say what you want, but you can't take the Sheffield Bed and Breakfast from me." Brenda raised her voice slightly to be heard through the closed door, not caring who overheard.

Ellen opened the door a crack, just wide enough to give Brenda another cold look. "You really must get used to the fact that it was never yours in the first place." She closed it again and Brenda heard the lock click.

When she composed herself and returned downstairs, the smell of the armfuls of flowers Allie and Jenny returned with became too much. "I need some fresh air. Jenny, the rest of the flowers should just go to the sitting room for now, I'll deal with them later. Allie, do you want a break?"

"Sure. Is the smell from all these flowers getting to you?"

Brenda thought her beautiful Sheffield house smelled like a funeral home but didn't express those thoughts aloud. "I could use a good walk right now."

They walked down the road toward Main Street. Brenda had never seen so many tourists at one time in Sweetfern Harbor. Not only were tourists visiting for the Seaside Theatre Festival, but reporters and journalists were in town for the duration of the show. Someone pointed out the owner of the Sheffield Bed and Breakfast right as they walked into town and Brenda found herself in the center of a small group of reporters clamoring for details about Ellen Teague.

As she listened to their silly questions, Brenda knew she had had enough of the actress. She finally said, "Please, I cannot divulge anything private about the star, or about any guest of the Sheffield. But I am sure Ellen will give interviews when ready." The disappointed reporters finally left her alone. Brenda and Allie finally reached Morning Sun Coffee in one piece and saw Shawn and Anna Quincy sitting at a table that looked out onto the street. Despite the indignities of hosting Ellen Teague, Brenda was determined that the other actors should have a better experience visiting their tiny town. Allie followed Brenda as she made her way to their table.

"I didn't get a chance to congratulate you both on your stunning performance last night. I thoroughly enjoyed the play and your acting was superb."

"Thank you. We're glad you enjoyed it," said Shawn, flashing her with one of his megawatt smiles. "Ricky has a few comp tickets that Ellen, or rather Chester, gave him if you want to see it again."

Brenda thanked him and told him she was busy, but she was sure Jenny wanted to go again. She didn't say it but privately she wondered if she could possibly enjoy seeing the play again. How could she enjoy seeing her formerly favorite actress on stage, pretending to be this glittering beauty of warmth and charm, when Brenda now knew what she was really like? She knew it wasn't something she was ready for. Shawn agreed he would pass the word on to Ricky to give the extra tickets to Jenny Rivers.

"You're welcome to join us," said Anna, patting the chair next to her and smiling at the still-starstruck Allie.

Brenda left her young employee happily chatting with the Hollywood stars and chatted with Molly, the proprietor, for a few minutes while she ordered their drinks. When their lattés were ready, Brenda carried them from the counter over to the table and sat down to listen as Anna finished telling Allie a hilarious story about a stage makeup mishap that had happened on her very first touring show.

As they finished their lattés, the cheery sound of the bell at the Morning Sun's door rang as more tourists trooped in. Brenda took that as their cue and told Allie they should get back to the bed and breakfast. They said their goodbyes to the Quincys and headed back on Main Street.

More than anything, Brenda reflected, she wanted to be alone. The town, crowded from the festival, began to suffocate her today as it never had before. It was not unlike the feeling she had felt in her bed and breakfast following the uncomfortable confrontation with Ellen. She had a lot to think about.

Upon their return, Brenda spoke to Phyllis and was relieved to hear there wouldn't be a repeat of yesterday's rehearsal on the back lawn. She decided to prepare her own lunch in the main kitchen and take it up the back stairway to her apartment. She needed time to think, but more than anything she hoped Edward Graham would call her soon. Perhaps he found a loophole of some sort or maybe he found out Ellen's claim was not legally sound after all.

Brenda had eaten her lunch and straightened her room when finally her phone rang. She glanced at the screen and saw it was Mac, and answered the call with some relief. He was eager to know if she had heard from Edward yet, and she gave him the disappointing news.

"Well, I'm sure he'll be in touch soon. Meanwhile, I thought I'd go see 'The Rich Game' again tonight. Jenny asked me to take her. She was sure caught up with it and she got complimentary tickets from Ricky Owens." He noted the pause from her end. "I didn't ask you since you gave me the impression you didn't like Ellen Teague so much now."

"It's perfectly fine. Your daughter wants to see it again and I'm not really interested. For the record, I still admire Ellen's talent but not so much her personality offstage. Have a good time tonight." She meant her last words, but she felt strange, almost lonely, knowing he didn't ask her first.

"I'm just being silly," she told herself when they had hung up. "Jenny really wants to see it again and why shouldn't Mac take her?"

In an attempt to distract herself, she thought again about the magnificent stories she had heard about her Uncle Randolph from the actors who had known him. What else did she not know about him? Could Ellen's claim have some merit? It was a troublesome thought.

She knew Randolph had married three times and never had a child of his own. The one time she had visited Sheffield house with her parents, her uncle had taken her up the narrow stairs to what she now knew was the attic. He showed her a playroom with a slanted ceiling and faded old wallpaper in a floral pattern. With a proud flourish, he opened the floor-to-ceiling cupboards to show her the old toys stored there, and then in the final cupboard he showed her a large antique dollhouse with all its furnishings. She had played with the delicate, tiny furniture and porcelain doll figures for hours while the adults talked downstairs. He seemed to find great happiness in her joy that day, like it was a secret he had been longing to share with just the right person. It was an enchanting memory, one she cherished. Not until she was in her teens had her parents mentioned him again, and only to mention how he had transformed the old mansion into a bed and breakfast. It wasn't until decades later that she learned he too never forgot his niece and that captivating visit to the attic playroom. After his death, her uncle's lawyer Edward Graham contacted her to inform her she was the heiress of his estate and now the proud owner of Randolph Sheffield's bed and breakfast.

Quiet descended on the Sheffield house as the day wore on into the late afternoon and still no phone call came from Edward. Brenda waited and finally drifted off to sleep in her chair and awoke with a start. Aside from the ticking of the hall clock, there was not a sound throughout the huge house. She remembered then that the cast and crew of the play had reserved dinner at one of the upscale restaurants at the edge of town with a waterfront view. It was time to discover who her uncle really was.

Brenda climbed the narrow stairs to the attic with a heavy-duty screwdriver in her hand. She switched on the light and walked through the first couple of empty rooms, toward the room farthest from the stairs where she knew her uncle's crates were stored. The revelation that he had once been an actor opened up a whole new chapter in his life as far as she was concerned. Even more fascinating to her was the fact that he had been connected to Ellen Teague, and that these crates could hold the key to that story.

Brenda opened the dusty room and brushed away a cobweb that hung from the light. She looked at the stacks of wooden crates and old-fashioned steam trunks before her. She lifted a crate down from one pile and read the handwritten note on the outside, "Costumes." Setting it down for later, she looked at the second crate which read, more promisingly, "Memorabilia." She pried open the top of the crate with her screwdriver, the nails squeaking in the wood, until she could take the lid off. Inside she found a treasure trove of Broadway tickets, advertising posters, and playbills. Randolph Sheffield's name was on everything. Brenda sat back on her heels in satisfaction.

"You really were an actor, Uncle Randolph. Why did I never know that?"

As hard as she tried, Brenda could not remember either parent talking about his days as an actor. As she sifted through several other boxes of memorabilia and other papers, Brenda found a small bundle of letters tied with a heavy string. The one on top was addressed to her father. It was stamped but had not been mailed. She turned it over and saw that it had not been sealed either. Perhaps Randolph had more to say and had never finished writing it. She unfolded the two sheets of paper and began reading.

In the letter, Randolph explained his frustrations to his brother, her father, Tim. Evidently this had been written during the run of a play in which he and Ellen Teague had been costars. Randolph wrote that he was tired of playing second fiddle to Ellen Teague. She hogged the spotlight until reporters started zeroing in on her alone. She played one character for the public, another character on the stage, and a nasty character in private, even in those days. She had played the press like a fiddle – so well, in fact, that her costar Randolph had barely merited a mention in the reviews that praised her talents and beauty. It had been a bitter pill to swallow for her uncle.

Brenda clutched the letter tighter, feeling a kinship through the years with her uncle. As she read on, she softened as she read that Randolph was in love with someone named Anne. No last name was provided in the letter. Ellen had snubbed him until she found out about Anne, and then Ellen found a million ways to sabotage him. She found ways to interrupt them, or show up when he was out on a date. She was not afraid to use her star power to try to ruin Randolph's chance at happiness.

In the last paragraph, Randolph told his brother he wanted out of show business. He missed the pleasures of living in a small town like the one the two brothers grew up in, in upstate New York. The next sentence began: *I have a chance to buy a historic home in a town called Sweetfern Harbor. I've visited there several times and have decided to purchase it. It is right on the...* here the words ended. This confirmed what Brenda thought: that her uncle had more to say or he would have mailed the letter to her father. She wondered what interrupted him and why he didn't go back and finish the letter. There was no way to answer that. The two brothers, along with her mother, were now deceased.

It dawned on her that she and her uncle were very much alike. He wanted a simpler life and so did she. When she had found out the bed and breakfast was hers, she discovered how much the town of Sweetfern Harbor and its life of simplicity and freedom drew her in. The townspeople had accepted her and it didn't take long for her to feel right at home for the first time in her life. She put her life as assistant to a Private Investigator back in Michigan aside. She had enjoyed her role as an amateur sleuth but was ready for peace and quiet in a quaint village set along the Atlantic Ocean. That didn't mean she would stop reading crime novels, though.

Whatever happened between Ellen Teague and Randolph Sheffield fed her curiosity. On the other hand, as hostess to the famous actress, she knew her first priority was to apologize to her guest for her behavior that morning and make things right again. She would have to set aside the terrible business of the court case and treat Ellen Teague just like any other guest.

Brenda closed up the attic again and returned to her room. She stretched out across her bed and flipped through an old script that she had come across in the crates. Immersed in the old-fashioned murder mystery play, she did not realize it was getting late until a cold breeze sailed through her curtains and made her shiver. She absently stayed awake reading until she heard everyone come in. She listened as doors closed and everyone started settling in for the night. Then she went down to Ellen's room and knocked on her door. Chester opened the door with expectant, raised eyebrows.

Brenda opened her mouth to speak but stopped when she heard another familiar voice. She looked past Chester and saw William Pendleton sitting in one of the wingback armchairs with a glass of champagne in his hand. Chester stepped aside as William turned to greet her, but Brenda chose to focus on Ellen.

"I'm sorry to interrupt, I just wanted to speak with Miss Teague. I can do that in the morning..."

"No, don't let me trouble you. I must be on my way," said William. Chester excused himself as well, saying he needed to see to the costumes that had been brought to his room.

Ellen looked down her nose at the interruption. "The costumes will have to be dry-cleaned again by tomorrow afternoon. It's our last performance here and I want them to look perfect."

"I'll let Allie know," said Brenda, as she watched William and Chester leave. She felt unaccountably nervous when she was left alone with Ellen. "I came to apologize for my bad behavior earlier. I hope you have found everything satisfactory during your stay here."

"I don't really care about your apology or anyone else's for that matter. If that is all, then I'll say goodnight—"

"That's not all. I was reading through my uncle's papers today. I only just found out that Randolph was an actor, and that you knew him, but I'm not sure how important you were to him at the time." Brenda knew she was only stirring up something she had come in to defuse but felt helpless to stop herself.

Ellen turned to regard Brenda silently for a moment before she said, "Randolph and I had a very...close relationship in those days. When he told me he was moving to Sweetfern Harbor I told him it was a huge mistake on his part. He was an actor with real talent but he threw it all away." For a moment, Brenda saw bitterness behind the actress's cool demeanor. "He always said he would turn this place into a bed and breakfast. I see that he reached his goal, though for the life of me I don't know why he would want to demean himself and his talents this way."

Ellen paused as if waiting for a certain reaction. Brenda

was determined not to give her the satisfaction of rising to the bait of such a hateful comment.

Instead, Brenda bit back her harsher words and replied evenly, "This is an honorable business – and a successful one I might add – and he recognized it as such. My uncle did much good around this community and was known as a mentor and benefactor."

Ellen waved her hand in dismissal of Brenda's words. "Never mind all of that. The people in a town like this couldn't possibly understand who he was truly meant to be. I spoke to Edward Graham again today. Once the Seaside Theatre Festival is finished and I'm back in New York I plan to file suit against the Sheffield estate for ownership of this establishment." Her chuckle bordered on a sneer. "Randolph promised me this house. And I don't plan to keep it in this sorry state, either. I plan to rehab the whole place and turn it back into a luxury estate for myself."

"Are you telling me that if you win this lawsuit, and you won't, that you will live here in Sweetfern Harbor?" Brenda could hardly believe her ears.

"Are you crazy? I don't plan on living here, but it will make a nice vacation home – perhaps one or two weeks in the summer. Who knows, I may discover what drove Randolph to choose this backwater town over me."

Brenda shook her head and fought to keep her anger at bay. She felt it seeping upward again, coloring her cheeks, and was powerless to hold her tongue. "You don't deserve this...this backwater. And you will never get this bed and breakfast, so don't count on it!"

She turned and swept out the door, slamming it behind her. It wasn't until she stood in the hall, fuming, that she realized the volume of her voice must have reached through the walls. She heard another soft chuckle through Ellen's closed door and the click of the lock.

Brenda's eyes swam with tears of frustration as she

returned to her apartment. But she refused to let those tears fall where anyone might see. The stress of the last few days overtook Brenda and as soon as she climbed into her own bed, her tears rolled down her cheeks until she finally turned over and sank into a fitful sleep.

chapter five

The next morning at breakfast, Brenda sat with Phyllis, who noticed her boss was quieter than usual.

"What's the matter, Brenda?"

Brenda shook her head. "It's something I have to figure out by myself and I plan to get right on it as soon as our guests leave for their final performance."

Phyllis gently prodded again but to no avail. She finally patted Brenda's arm and told her when she was ready to talk about it she would be there for her. The two women sat in the quiet of the morning, gazing at the crystal-clear view of the Atlantic Ocean from the window of the sitting room as they enjoyed their coffee. Neither had a hint of what was to come only moments later when Shawn Quincy burst into the room with his fatal news.

"She's dead."

After Brenda had entered the room and found Ellen Teague motionless atop her bed, she ushered the curious actors away, instructed Chester to let no one near the room, and quickly returned to the first floor. As she called 911 from the front desk and told the dispatcher to send an ambulance, she looked across the hall into the sitting room only to see Shawn Quincy sitting in an armchair as Phyllis patted his shoulder soothingly. The actor was expressionless and Brenda supposed he must have been in mild shock.

In a short time, she heard the wail of sirens as they approached the bed and breakfast. Mac Rivers was the first one through the door, and he gave Brenda a quick, worried look as she led him and the paramedic crew up to Ellen's door. The other actors stood in a group a few feet away in the hallway. Allie and Phyllis remained rooted at the top of the stairs. No one spoke a word. The ambulance crew rushed in behind the detective and Brenda. She watched as the two paramedics quickly checked the actress for vital signs. She had no pulse, no breath, and the body was already cold, so resuscitation would have no effect. The lead paramedic shook her head ruefully.

"I'm calling it in," she said. She examined the inert body on the bed again. "I'll get the coroner here." She turned away to make a phone call.

Brenda watched Mac closely and saw him looking at Ellen's body and her surroundings with the practiced eye of a detective. She looked around too and several details were immediately apparent. Empty champagne glasses were scattered on the two small bedside tables. It looked as if Ellen finished off the bottle after everyone left her room the night before. There was a belt Brenda recognized from the green satin dressing gown she wore the evening before when they had their unpleasant encounter. The belt dangled loosely from the corner post of the bed. Red marks stood out lividly on the ashen flesh of Ellen's throat.

"Looks like strangulation," said Mac. "I'd say that belt could be the weapon. Doesn't look like hands did it, but of course that's up to the coroner to decide."

Brenda nodded in agreement with Mac's assessment. The overwhelming odor of the bouquets and vases of flowers caused a sickened lurch in the pit of Brenda's stomach. The windows were shut tight and the air in the room was uncomfortably warm. Brenda itched to open a window but knew she couldn't touch anything.

Mac continued to walk around the room. He pulled on gloves and fingered a card in a plastic holder sticking out of an especially large vase of red roses. Brenda stepped closer to examine it alongside him.

"Read this," he said. Brenda saw the words 'Good Riddance' on the card. There was no signature.

Mac motioned for another officer who had arrived with him and asked him to put the note in a bag and to gather any other evidence he could find. "Take that vase of roses, too. And the shiny green belt, of course."

They heard the coroner arrive – in the strange quiet that had descended on the bed and breakfast, Brenda could discern each voice downstairs as Allie ushered him in. The coroner arrived with a photographer assistant who took a number of photographs during the coroner's examination. It didn't take long for him to pronounce her dead and to fill out the appropriate paperwork. Not much longer after that, the paramedics brought their gurney to the room and took out an extra sheet to wrap the body for privacy from the prying eyes of the public who had gathered on the sidewalk outside. Brenda watched, half in shock, as Ellen's body was wheeled out to the ambulance for transportation to the morgue.

Mac touched Brenda's arm gently and searched her eyes for reassurance.

"Brenda, I need your help. No one is allowed to leave the premises until we have interviewed them all." Brenda nodded, firmly pushing away the shocking events and vowing to focus on supporting Mac. "Are there other guests here besides the actors?"

Brenda told him of the two regulars. The couple had peeked into the hall during the commotion and their faces had paled when Ellen's body was taken away. The woman had turned and Brenda had distinctly heard her lose her breakfast. The husband hurriedly closed the door and they had not emerged since.

"The officer will be dusting for fingerprints and gathering as much evidence as possible. It won't be the last search in here, so please inform your staff and the other guests that the room is strictly off limits." Brenda nodded. He walked toward Chester who had not moved from his post in the doorway of his room since the body had been wheeled out of the room. His face was hard to read, but, Brenda reflected, that was no different than it had been since his arrival. "Mr. Boyd, I will begin with you. Let's go to your room where we can talk in private."

Chester stepped into his room and Mac followed him as an officer strung yellow crime scene tape across the hallway door to Ellen's room. Mac was surprised to see that Chester's room had an interior door with direct access to Ellen's room. He was satisfied he chose the assistant as his first interviewee. He offered his condolences to Chester and opened with a few easy questions about their stay at Sheffield Bed and Breakfast so far, and the star's daily routines. Then he got right to the point.

"When did you last see Ellen Teague?"

"I last saw her alive late last night, around eleven o'clock. She had a guest in her room and the three of us drank champagne to celebrate the success of the play. The guest left when Miss Sheffield came to speak with Miss Teague. I left for my room before they spoke. Before I could get into bed I had to get the costumes bundled up for dry-cleaning. Miss Sheffield had arranged for that per Miss Teague's orders."

The detective noted that Chester's face hardly betrayed any emotion. He reflected that perhaps the actress's assistant was in shock, as often happened to close associates of a murder victim. Mac asked if he knew why the owner of the bed and breakfast came to Ellen's room so late at night.

"I presume to check if there was anything else Miss Teague needed. We had just returned after the performance. Miss Sheffield has been very good about making sure we are all taken care of." When asked, Chester told Mac the guest who visited was William Pendleton. "He came in to visit and congratulate her on the performance. They had met before and so were acquainted."

"That's all my questions for now. I am very sorry for your loss, but no one is allowed to leave the premises," said Mac. "I will want to question you again, I'm sure."

"We'll all be right here. There is one final performance before we leave town."

"So the play won't be canceled in light of her death?" Mac was surprised to hear this.

"Oh, no, the show will go on. That's how it always is."

"Who will play Miss Teague's part?" asked Mac.

"I suppose it will be Bonnie or possibly Anna. Ricky will figure out how to make it all work." Chester sat on his bed with his hands calmly folded as Mac thanked him and walked out of the room.

Mac walked away shaking his head. He had enjoyed the play but was shocked that the show would go on even after the star's death. But seeing Chester's calm demeanor, he didn't doubt it would. Mac looked for Brenda again and gave her a nod. She stood talking to Phyllis and Allie, but turned to address the actors who stood milling around the second-floor hallway.

"Everyone please go downstairs for a late breakfast. I know this has been a difficult morning, but Detective Rivers will want to speak to each one of you. Please don't leave the premises until he says it's all right to do so."

The cast was subdued and in shock. Brenda studied each

face as they passed her. Nothing gave her any ideas of who did this. When she reflected on the strained relationship between Ellen and the other cast members, there was no doubt in her mind that any of them would be relieved to have her gone – but dead? It seemed unthinkable. But the killer was clearly among them. She turned when Mac called to her.

"Who found the body?"

She walked over to where he stood looking through his notes. "Shawn Quincy. He told Phyllis that he went into her room to fetch a script. The door was unlocked and she didn't answer, so he assumed she was already down at breakfast. But Mac, wouldn't Chester have heard him knocking?"

"Chester told me he always waited for her to call for him in the mornings. When she was ready for him, she would call for him to enter, but he was never to go in until then."

Brenda paused, thinking. "Did the coroner determine time of death?"

"That's the puzzling part. He said he couldn't give a precise time until after his full examination, but based on the temperature of her body she had been dead for quite a few hours. What happened when you spoke to her last night?"

"I tried to apologize about something I said, but it didn't go over too well. I was angry and slammed the door on the way out. She locked it. I heard the latch turn."

Mac stopped and stared at her. "You and Ellen Teague argued last night? What was that all about?"

Brenda held her breath for a moment as she realized this must sound suspicious. "I came to her room after everyone got back, to apologize for an earlier argument I had with her. You have to understand, she said terrible things about my uncle and she still claims the bed and breakfast was meant for her. I lost my temper the first time and came to apologize for my bad behavior, hoping to put it behind us. Instead, she just insisted she would file suit against the estate to get Sheffield Bed and Breakfast." Brenda looked down, afraid to meet his eyes. "I'm afraid I shouted at her and told her she would never get it. I'm sorry. It was the wrong thing to do."

Mac decided to store this information in the back of his head for now, but it troubled him. "What's more important is that we need to find out who unlocked Ellen Teague's door. If we can answer this question, we'll be well on our way." Brenda nodded in relief and agreement and followed him down the stairs. When the detective and owner walked into the dining room, the cast were discussing details of the last performance of "The Rich Game."

"I know every line," Chester was saying. "I can be the country estate host, instead of a hostess, freeing up Bonnie to take over Ellen's part." Ricky chimed in that he agreed it was the most logical solution. Brenda noticed a curious lack of tears among the actors, though Bonnie sat quietly stirring her mug of tea and not joining in the conversation, despite the favorable new casting decision.

Mac singled out Shawn Quincy and led him away from the table and asked Brenda to join them. They went into the sitting room where they closed the doors in order to speak privately.

"Do you have any idea who may have unlocked Miss Teague's room sometime early this morning or perhaps last night?"

"I have no idea," said Shawn. "Every cast member has a key to the room." Brenda's head jerked up at this detail, which was news to her. "Ellen told Chester to have keys made for all of us so we would have access in case she was out. If the room was unlocked, we knew that meant someone else had already been in there and it was all right for the rest of us to do the same. I don't know who went in first."

Inwardly, Brenda seethed thinking of the lack of concern for safety Ellen Teague had displayed by her actions, to say nothing of her audacity to copy keys without permission. She made a mental note to have the lock changed on that door once the investigation was completed.

After questioning, Shawn stated he had been in his room with his wife all night once they were back at the bed and breakfast.

"Did either of you leave the room at all once you arrived back here?"

"Anna left for maybe twenty minutes to use the Wi-Fi in the lobby. She had to email her agent in New York City," he said. "She mentioned talking briefly with Allie. I'm sure she will vouch for Anna. I watched TV for a while until she got back. That was around ten o'clock. I remember the time since neither of us was interested in watching the news. We were bushed and decided to get a good night's sleep."

"Is there anyone who can vouch for you that you didn't leave the room while your wife was downstairs?"

The actor looked taken aback momentarily. "Well, no, I was alone until she returned. As I said, I watched TV until she came back." He glanced at Brenda. "Both of us woke up when we heard you and Ellen. We laughed since it was rare that anyone stood up to her like that." He quickly amended his words. "We didn't know what was said but it sounded as if you were winning."

Brenda felt a flush rise to her face. "I apologize for my behavior, and for awakening you."

Shawn smiled, evidently still savoring the experience of overhearing Ellen's comeuppance, and waved her apology aside. Mac looked at Brenda's flushed cheeks. It was unnerving to hear about the argument again. Mac shook his head at the impossible thoughts that came to him. He excused Shawn from the interview and thanked him for his time.

"I guess his words will have to be taken as truth for now," said Brenda. "There is no one except his wife to say he stayed there all night long. That's a question to ask the others. Maybe someone saw if anybody left their rooms in the middle of the night."

"That's true. We have to take his word for now. And of course we'll have the fingerprints from Ellen's room."

"Yes, but I'm sure he will find mine and the fingerprints of the staff who clean in there. And there will be every cast member's prints, including Chester's. Not only were members of the show coming and going for costumes but their scripts and some of the smaller props were in there as well."

Mac took a breath and held it before letting it escape. "You are right about that. Everyone who has been in that room is a suspect." He called to Allie who was leaving the desk. She confirmed the alibi Shawn gave for his wife.

"If Shawn heard you when his wife got back upstairs then he couldn't have done it while she was gone. She obviously was still alive at that point." Mac paced a few steps, still bothered by his nagging thoughts. He turned to look at Brenda with tension furrowing his brow. "How angry were the two of you to be yelling like that?"

"I told you exactly what happened," Brenda said. She felt herself shut down. She realized that Mac looked at her as a possible suspect. After all they had gone through, he did not trust her word. The blow she felt in that moment was as if he had physically knocked her to the floor.

Sooner or later, he would question her. She did not know if she could bear to hear those doubts spoken out loud. She closed her eyes for a brief moment and touched the promise ring on her finger.

Mac was still intent on his thought process and continued to pace. "Did William Pendleton visit Ellen more than the one time you observed him?"

Brenda forced herself to answer normally, though she could feel herself wanting to run away or panic. "I don't know if he did or not. He could have. This is a big place and

I'm not always at the entrance or on this floor for that matter. My guests relax and interact as they wish."

"I will interview him next. He may have a clue I can go on. Maybe he saw someone heading upstairs when he left."

"He was in her room when I came in. He should be interviewed as you are doing everyone else."

Mac noted her set jawline. She was savvy enough to know he had to consider her as a suspect along with everyone else. "I will talk with William Pendleton. I have my doubts he was involved in a murder...but I'll have to get to him after I deal with your guests."

Brenda knew Mac admired William. After the death of William's wife, he had been very benevolent toward the people of Sweetfern Harbor. Mac Rivers was devoted to his town and often commented on how peaceful things had become after William had gained control of the wealth of properties that had been controlled by his greedy, unhappy wife before her death.

Brenda turned away and mumbled she would see Mac later. She felt sure if she stayed another moment, he would probably just ask her to leave in case she influenced the investigation. And it was agony to see the man she loved extend the benefit of doubt to William Pendleton but not to her own circumstances. But she resolutely refused to dwell on this. She went to the office to check with Allie on who the next guests would be when the cast of "The Rich Game" left. If the play would go on as normal, then so would the Sheffield Bed and Breakfast.

chapter six

Mac Rivers asked Phyllis for a cup of coffee and wearily flipped through his notes. It had been a long morning already and it was still not over. Luckily, William Pendleton had shown up at the bed and breakfast without even being called. He had come to support Phyllis, and had easily agreed to wait with the actors for his own turn to be interviewed. Mac signaled William from the small group waiting in the dining room. He realized he still expected to see Brenda behind him but she was nowhere in sight. He sat across from William in the sitting room and asked him to recount his movements of the night before until this morning.

"Phyllis and I walked back here after the performance ended. It was a beautiful night. We both like to walk on these lovely summer nights. We went directly to her apartment in the back of the bed and breakfast." William smiled fondly. "I've tried to get her to move in with me – that rambling house I live in is too big for just one person and needs a woman's touch – but she likes her independence. It may take time, but I'll convince her soon to marry me." He appeared to drift off in his thoughts until Mac drew him back in with another question.

"How long were you with Phyllis?"

"Perhaps twenty minutes? She brought out cups of tea and cookies and we enjoyed that until we heard the actors come in at the front door. Her oatmeal raisin cookies are hard to resist but I wanted to congratulate the cast before everyone headed to bed. Phyllis said she was tired and had seen them every day since their arrival anyway. To be honest, Mac, I was glad she stayed behind. I was drawn to Ellen in a lot of ways. She was a great actress and not bad to look at."

Mac's eyes cast a look of frank disbelief at the older gentleman.

"Oh no, it was nothing like that," William added hastily. "Phyllis is my true love. But I admire Ellen, and we had met on several occasions. We conversed easily together unlike many who found her too aloof. She called Chester in to open champagne. She was in quite a celebratory mood. The three of us sat down and were drinking it when Brenda came to the door. Any alcohol makes me sleepy right away. I used to be able to handle it better. When Brenda came to the door it gave me an excuse to leave before I fell asleep right there. I didn't see Phyllis again since she told me she was going to bed after I left for Ellen's room."

"Did you see anyone in the hallways when you left?"

He shook his head no. "Everyone must have been in their rooms, I assumed. By then, it was close to eleven or after."

"Did you see anyone around the office or front entrance on your way out?"

Again, his answer was in the negative. Mac excused him to go home if he wanted and next he asked Ricky Owens to join him in the sitting room. The actor's light brown hair matched his neatly trimmed beard. Mac assessed his age to be near his own early forties. He was aware that this actor was well-known in the theatre world. The detective had done his homework and found that Ricky Owens had won many acting awards. He had also been acclaimed since being cast in several roles opposite Ellen Teague. He reached for Mac's hand and the firm handshake was sure. Mac gestured for him to sit down and was impressed that Ricky, like the other actors, appeared well in control of his emotions despite the events of that morning. But he immediately wished to have a second set of eyes to confirm his impressions of the actor.

"If you don't mind, I'd like to have Brenda in here on these interviews. Excuse me for a moment and I'll find her." Mac walked out into the hall, thinking back to the look on Brenda's face before she had left the room earlier.

Brenda walked out of the office just as Mac came out of the sitting room. He asked her to join him again. "I thought you were going to stay with me during these interviews. I need your input." His eyes teased a little. "You are good at this, Brenda. You know I've always admired you for your investigative work back in Michigan."

This gave Brenda the boost to her ego she needed after the incident earlier between them, so she swallowed her fears and rejoined him. They all three settled comfortably in the paisley chairs. Brenda was happy that Mac trusted her enough to keep her around for the interviews, after all. Perhaps she had overreacted to his earlier remarks.

"I want to hear what you did after you arrived back here last night, Mr. Owens," said Mac.

"It had been a long night. Our fans swarmed around wanting autographs after the show. Ellen of course liked to keep the crowds there for as long as possible." Ricky laughed softly. "The truth was that Ellen loved to bask in her glory. She had the habit of pushing the rest of us aside when someone asked for an autograph. She would then scribble her name on whatever the fan pushed toward her. Ellen was like that. She always had to be in the limelight." He grinned. "It's just the way she is – was. It was irritating to all of us at times, but what could we do?"

Brenda bit her lip. With Ricky's joking attitude it was hard to tell if Ellen's "irritating" habits were really the full story. "When you got home, what did you do next?" she asked.

"I went straight to bed. We had one last performance coming up and I was too exhausted to celebrate with anyone. Besides, we usually have a bigger celebration in New York after the last show. But I guess Ellen was celebrating. I saw the champagne glasses."

Brenda and Mac stared at him. "Have you been in her room since her death?" Mac asked.

"I haven't been in there at all. I knew my costume wouldn't be ready until early afternoon. I saw the champagne remnants from the open doorway while we all waited out in the hall. It was while the coroner was in her room."

"Can you say for sure you did not leave your room once you settled in last night?" asked Mac.

"There is no one to vouch for me, but I can say for sure I did not leave my room once I arrived back here. I admit I was still awake when I heard loud voices coming from her room." He didn't mention Brenda's voice in particular, for which she was grateful.

When Ricky Owens left the sitting room, Mac and Brenda discussed the fact that there was no real way to prove whether Ricky Owens was in bed all night long, and alone, or not. He seemed to be upfront and honest. He certainly didn't hold back on how the others felt about Ellen Teague's ego and leadership style. But despite his smooth and polite exterior, Brenda couldn't help but think that Ricky was holding something back.

Bonnie Ross was next in line for an interview. Brenda had been paying close attention to everyone's hands. Ricky's had been sinewy and strong looking. Shawn Quincy's hands were slender and more refined from years of training as a dancer. She looked at Bonnie's hands as the young woman settled herself into the chair in front of her. Overall, she was a bit overweight but curvy and with delicate features. Her hands with their delicate pink manicured nails didn't look strong enough to wield a belt around someone's neck enough to strangle them. Brenda realized that the murderer would have to be strong enough to manage it without letting Ellen making a sound to alert her assistant through the adjoining door.

Why hadn't Chester heard anything? Brenda recalled how often she had witnessed him responding to Ellen when she called for him, no matter how far away from her he was.

"I was in bed asleep the whole night," said Bonnie as Mac began the questioning. "I was so excited, but a girl needs her beauty sleep. This is my first play and to be working with Ellen Teague is icing on the cake." She laughed and then blushed. "That is – it was. I can't believe she's gone."

"How did you personally feel about Ellen?" Bonnie drew back a little at the penetrating gaze the detective gave her.

"I reveled in the chance to act on stage right next to someone as talented and well-known as Ellen. I know the other actors complained about her, called her narcissistic. I don't deny that she wasn't always easy to work with but I tried not to let it bother me."

"Did you hear anything unusual in the middle of the night?" Mac asked.

Bonnie shot a wide-eyed glance toward Brenda and hesitated.

"Go ahead and tell us everything," Brenda said, knowing what caused her hesitation.

"Well, I heard arguing in the hall. I think I had been asleep maybe an hour or so. It was your voice, Brenda, right? I heard you and Ellen arguing. That's what woke me up, but once things settled down again I was back into a deep sleep."

Brenda expressed an apology to her guest for the disturbance. Bonnie waved it off. "You weren't the first person to argue with Ellen," she said with a dimpled smile, "but I have to admit I believe you were the first to get the last word in."

After Bonnie was excused, Mac looked at Brenda with an unreadable expression. "It seems your argument with Ellen Teague left quite an impression." Brenda was once more chagrined and looked away from the man she loved, trying to gather her thoughts.

"Mac, no one here doubts my commitment to the Sheffield Bed and Breakfast..." she paused and swallowed nervously, trying to gain courage. "I'm happy to answer any questions you have for me, at any time." He nodded and thanked her for being so open, but privately he still wondered.

Mac shuffled his notes and left the room to fetch Anna Quincy. She was the only guest remaining to be interviewed before they would proceed to speak with Brenda's staff members Phyllis Lindsey and Allie Williams. Mac knew he also needed to interview Chester Boyd again. He had no reason to suspect him in particular, but the assistant knew the star better than anyone else, to say nothing of his easy access to her room.

"Did you like Ellen Teague?" Mac directed his first question to Anna when she was settled in the sitting room with him and Brenda.

"I admired her and was grateful she cast me in the plays she helped produce and direct and star in, but as for liking her, Ellen was not an easy person to like."

"I would think if she continued to give you important parts that you could overlook her shortcomings." Brenda kept her eyes on Anna for a reaction, but the young actress held her gaze with seeming honesty and openness.

"To be honest with you, I had an argument with her only an hour before the performance yesterday. She knew I was good in this role, it was a bigger and better part than I'd had the chance to act in before. But she told me that in the next play I would have a very minor role. I was very unhappy to hear that from her and we argued back and forth a little bit... I felt almost as if she tried to start a fight with me just before the performance to throw me off my game." Brenda couldn't help but wonder if anyone else had witnessed that particular argument.

When questioned further, Anna explained that Ellen was fond of typecasting her as the dumb blonde in the stage comedies she liked to produce back in New York. "I only took those parts to get ahead, not to make a career out of them. Shawn told me Ellen knew I was good and didn't want me to outshine her."

Brenda found that assessment eerily similar to the behavior her Uncle Randolph had described from many years ago. It seemed that sabotage was Ellen's specialty, and she had only gotten better at it as her fame and career had advanced. After Mac dismissed Anna, he turned to Brenda. "What do you think?"

"I think she had motive. Maybe she and Shawn did it together. I've seen how protective he is of Anna." Brenda reminded Mac of the incident they had witnessed in Harbor Park after the performance on opening night. "The press and all those fans were heading toward Shawn and Anna too until Ellen walked out. She stole the spotlight from the other actors in there. It appears none of them liked her but held on to move careers ahead." She stood up to go. "I think that's the last of them. You did interview the couple staying in the far wing, didn't you?"

"I ruled them out. We'll fingerprint them too, but I'm sure they had nothing to do with it. They are shaken up over the whole incident." Mac tapped his pen on his notepad absently and she suddenly knew what he was waiting to ask. "I need to ask you questions now, too, Brenda. You knew this was coming." Brenda nodded and sat back down. "Your relationship was certainly strained once you found out that

Ellen meant to take the Sheffield Bed and Breakfast away from you."

Brenda stared at him. "I told you everything I know about that – Edward never called me so I don't know if he found out anything more. I told you about the argument that everyone seems to have heard. It was bad timing, but it was just an argument. And I don't deny it. But I didn't step foot in that room until Shawn came to tell me she was dead. Are you calling me a suspect?"

"Everyone is a suspect, Brenda. And especially anyone who had a motive and you did have motive." Mac told her he was on his way to see Edward Graham. "I have to find out more details about the case against you and the Sheffield estate."

He didn't deny she was a suspect. She could feel her heart pounding in her chest painfully.

"You really don't know me at all, do you Mac Rivers?" Brenda rolled the promise ring around on her finger. "If you did, you would be looking for the real killer."

"I have to look at everyone." He stood and left without saying goodbye, aware of the awkwardness of the situation.

After he left to go to the lawyer's office, she took the ring off and slipped it into her pocket.

Mac drove his squad car to Edward Graham's office as fast as he could safely allow himself to go, but his mind was racing even faster. The more Mac thought about the events between Brenda and Ellen, the more he seethed. How could he be questioning someone he was sure he was in love with? Had he been falling for a woman capable of murder? He parked and hurried into the lawyer's office. Tracy, Edward's paralegal, told him Mr. Graham was working at his desk. When she buzzed his office, he told her to send Mac in.

"Edward, I need to know the details of the lawsuit against Brenda and the Sheffield estate. It may have bearing on a murder investigation." Mac's jaw tensed as Edward turned to regard him seriously.

"It's true that Ellen Teague was bent on suing for ownership of the Sheffield Bed and Breakfast. In fact, Ellen had an appointment with me today to deliver the final version of the lawsuit against the Sheffield estate, she had her lawyer in New York draw it up before she came to town, evidently. She had already brought me a draft of it...she told me she wanted to get it moving along before she left for New York City after the last performance."

"I need details of that lawsuit."

Edward opened his computer and then printed a hard copy. He handed it to the detective. "Ellen was adamant that Randolph promised her the establishment. In the lawsuit, she states that she was to retrieve proof of his promise and provide it in court. She swore she had proof of his intentions."

"But I thought his will named Brenda as his sole heir."

"You're correct. I took care of that for Randolph and notified Brenda as soon as the will was to be read. The question is, what date is on the so-called proof Ellen Teague had? If it was after the will, then Ellen's claim perhaps would have been a strong one." Edward tilted his chair back and clasped his hands behind his head. "Ellen was determined to fight her case in court."

"She didn't appear to be someone who would enjoy running a bed and breakfast."

Edward laughed ruefully. "She didn't plan to keep it as a business. In fact, I don't believe she was as interested in owning the place as much as she was in winning it from Brenda. Ours was not a pleasant meeting. She hinted that she and Randolph didn't part on good terms once he decided to leave show business."

"Then why would he give it to her?"

"According to Ellen, it was a token of their former relationship. A promise made because he naively hoped she would join him in his love of Sweetfern Harbor. But Randolph must have forgotten all about it, if what she says is true. This is all an act of revenge of some sort on her part."

Detective Rivers felt torn, learning all this from Edward. He hated to think of Brenda losing the Sheffield Bed and Breakfast, but he had to admit that it seemed like a very strong motivation. As he returned to his car, he knew he needed to talk with Brenda again. The more he thought about her, the more he wondered if she had made one very bad decision following that argument, and was now using her connection to him to cover her tracks. Her motives were stronger than anyone interviewed so far. Furthermore, she had the strength to do it. He had seen her lift furniture and other heavy objects when rearranging rooms in the bed and breakfast. He had visited one day to help with a small renovation project and had been surprised to see Brenda was so strong. She handled heavy armchairs as if they were light as a feather.

chapter seven

Mac drove to the bed and breakfast and asked Allie to get Brenda. When she came from the kitchen area, he suggested they sit out in the rose garden to continue their talk. Brenda didn't miss his serious expression and thought she denoted a note of sadness in his eyes when he looked at her. She fingered the ring in her pocket as she followed him to the garden and they sat down at a bench under the rose arbor.

"I've talked with Edward Graham. He gave me details of the lawsuit Ellen's lawyer prepared. I read part of it. Her lawyer stated that she has proof that Randolph promised her the property and she would provide that proof in court."

Brenda raised her eyes to meet Mac's with dread. "Was it dated before or after the date on the will?"

"Edward never got to see the proof. Ellen was to send a copy of it as soon as she got back."

"How do we know my uncle actually gave it to her? It doesn't make sense. I didn't tell you this before, but I found one of my uncle's letters in the attic, he told my father he wanted out of show business because of Ellen Teague and the way she treated him. He resented her because she hogged the spotlight and sabotaged him, and he didn't get recognized for his talent even when he was a costar alongside her."

"When did you find that letter?"

"I searched through his crates of belongings in the attic the other night when you took your daughter to the second performance of the play. It was after I found out from the actors that Randolph had been an actor and director. I was clueless that he had a theatre career and I wanted to find out more about him. That's when I found the letter. It was unfinished. He wrote it to my father but never mailed it. In it, he said he couldn't take Ellen Teague any longer. I don't know exactly what that was about, but those were his words. Honestly, I think I know exactly how he felt, too..." Brenda turned to look at Mac as she trailed off, and was horrified to see the cloud of suspicion on his face grow darker.

"Brenda, you continue to prove to me your motives are strongest for wanting her dead. You were upset with her treatment of your uncle and at the same time you had everything to lose. Isn't it true that once Ellen Teague was dead, you had no worries? You get to keep the bed and breakfast and you don't have to face a fight in court. You are an amateur sleuth, and a very good one I might add. Just the kind of person who might know how to hide her tracks. And you are dating the head detective." He finished bitterly, not looking at her.

Brenda jumped to her feet and glared at Mac. She stuffed her hand into her pocket for the ring and it sprang out, falling to the ground. The promise ring bounced on the brick walkway and made a sound like a sad little bell. She retrieved it and pressed it into his hand.

"I don't know what this so-called promise ring meant to you, Mac Rivers, but obviously it meant nothing. If you truly loved me you would know I am not capable of murder. I'm a fighter and I would have gone to court over this and fought with everything I had to defend my uncle's legacy. But I would never, ever commit murder. Not even to get what rightfully belongs to me in the first place." Rage shot through her body. "You are wasting your time with me. Arrest me if you have more questions. I suggest you go interview the actors again if you want to find the real murderer." Brenda whirled on her heel and left the rose garden.

As she walked away, he replied quietly to her retreating form, just loud enough for her to hear, "I can give you one day, Brenda. One day."

She picked up her pace until she reached the back door of the bed and breakfast. Just inside, she saw Phyllis and chef Morgan turn from the window where they had been watching her wrathful entrance.

"What was that all about?" Phyllis asked.

Brenda shook her head violently and stalked down the hallway to the back stairs and continued up the stairs at a furious pace. Phyllis and Morgan turned to look at each other in consternation, then Phyllis followed her. At the top of the stairs she hesitated and then kept walking to catch up to Brenda. When Phyllis entered the farthest attic room, she found Brenda pulling stacks of papers from a large crate. Her eyes were rimmed with red but not a tear spilled on her cheeks.

"Brenda, you can trust me. Tell me what is going on."

"Mac considers me his top suspect in the murder of Ellen Teague." She bent back to the crate and yanked out another handful of papers and sorted through them quickly.

"How can he begin to think that?" Phyllis replied in shock.

"I don't know, but he does." Brenda interspersed her tale of the recent events with Mac in between sorting through the mess of papers arrayed around her. When she finished she barely suppressed the sobs that tried to bubble to the surface. She looked at the empty crates and sat back on her heels. "Help me go through all of this. Please, Phyllis. Look for anything that has Ellen Teague's name on it. I don't care if it is a ticket, a theatre bill, a letter, a legal document. Anything. There's got to be something here that can help me."

They dug in silence for a while. Brenda sputtered more words, still finding it hard to believe she found herself in this situation. "He has given me a day to solve this murder case and then he will issue a warrant for my arrest."

This time Phyllis gasped. "He's gone crazy. There are plenty of actors who arrived with Ellen who intensely disliked her. Any of them could have had a motive, but not you, Brenda. He should know better than that." She hugged Brenda. "Maybe he's just frustrated that he has no solid leads and is taking it out on you. I don't mean to excuse him for his behavior but it may explain some things."

"No one solves a murder case this complicated in two days," Brenda said. "He knows that. After all, he is the detective and I'd like to see him solve cases that fast."

Phyllis didn't say it but she figured that in Mac's mind, he had solved the case. Brenda felt rather than saw Phyllis stop what she was doing. She knew Phyllis's eyes were glued to her.

"Why does Mac see you as the prime suspect?"

"Before her death, Ellen met with Edward Graham and told him she planned to file a lawsuit against me for ownership of the bed and breakfast. She claims that Randolph promised her this place. The draft of the lawsuit Edward received stated that she had proof in New York and planned to send it immediately to Edward once she arrived back home."

"And that's all Mac has to go on?" Phyllis narrowed her eyes as she pondered this. "It seems to me that Ellen would have brought that proof with her if she had it."

Brenda flashed her housekeeper a grateful look. "I agree. But also – our guests heard me arguing with Ellen about her preposterous claims the night she was killed."

"Well, I'm still baffled. He needs to get past his suspicions once and for all. We are all behind you, Brenda. You can count on Sweetfern Harbor. I'll get Molly on it along with her friends. My daughter has a steady run of customers in Morning Sun Coffee every day. She also told me the actors often talk freely when they are there. Allie will help, and her mother will listen to her customers, too, in case she overhears something useful. Everyone goes in for goodies from Hope Williams's bakery."

Brenda began to feel better. Phyllis was right. Sweetfern Harbor was a tight-knit family and Brenda could count on support as she raced against the clock. In the meantime, she would conduct her own line of questioning with her guests. She didn't bother wasting time wondering why Mac hadn't interviewed everyone a second time before fastening onto his suspicions that her motive was the strongest. The blood rushing through her changed from livid anger to determination. She thought about Jenny Rivers, who was Mac's daughter, but also a close friend to many in the community. Brenda wondered if Jenny would take Brenda's side or the side of her detective father.

It didn't take long for word to spread among friends and Jenny called Brenda as soon as she heard, outraged at her father. "Don't worry, Brenda, I will personally help you prove him wrong. I've always been good at getting people to talk without them realizing how much they are saying." Brenda had to chuckle. Jenny did have a way of charming information from unsuspecting people while they perused the florist shop. She thanked Jenny and was relieved to feel that she had such strong support even from Mac's daughter. Brenda quickly asked Jenny what she knew about any suspicious messages delivered with flower bouquets, but the florist said it must not have come from her shop. Perhaps it had been one of the many bouquets thrown onstage at the close of the performance, and so it was impossible to tell where it had come from.

Now that the town was on her side, she focused on her guests. She had two hours before they would leave for the park to perform one last time in Sweetfern Harbor with the Seaside Theatre Festival before it toured back to New York City. She gathered them all together and told them she wanted to speak with them again. Though it was unorthodox, she chose to have them all together. She wanted to observe their reactions to one another and to pick up any innuendo they might exchange between themselves.

"Where's Chester?" she asked, as she realized the group was short one person.

"We thought you wanted to talk with the cast only," Ricky said with surprise.

"He's a cast member now," Anna pointed out. "He's going to play the country estate host so Bonnie can take Ellen's part. I guess we forgot, we're so used to him being an assistant to..." Anna didn't seem to want to even say the late actress's name.

Shawn went upstairs to find Chester. He came down alone, shrugging his shoulders at Brenda. "He is nowhere to be found. He must have taken a walk into town."

Brenda thought perhaps it would be better to have a one-on-one with Chester, so she let it go for the moment. She told them she wanted to hear their accounts of the evening before, when everyone had returned to the bed and breakfast. She began with Bonnie, who eagerly repeated the same story she told Brenda and Mac. One by one Brenda asked the others, and they stuck to their stories.

"Did you and Anna go to sleep right around ten or so?" she asked Shawn.

"We were sound asleep as soon as our heads hit the pillows," he said. He smiled. "We woke up when we heard you yelling at Ellen." Despite the actress's death, he appeared to still see humor in the incident. "None of us ever got the last word with her like that," said Shawn. That's all it took for the rest of the group to smile, as well. Brenda was still shocked at their lack of sadness at Ellen Teague's death, and she began to wonder if perhaps all of them had planned the murder together. They were actors, after all. Perhaps they were so good at acting they were hiding their true intentions. She could only hope that repeated questions would trip them up, if so.

After an hour of questions and verifying little details, Brenda was disappointed to discover nothing out of place with any of their stories. She wished them well on the last performance. "I hope you still have a good turnout tonight."

"Oh, I think we'll have a bigger crowd than ever," said Ricky with a smirk. "The tabloids are all over Ellen's death and there's probably just as many gawkers as there are theatre fans with tickets tonight. I heard ticket scalpers are making a pretty penny down on Main Street."

As the rest of the actors turned to leave to get ready for the performance, Brenda pulled Shawn and Anna aside briefly. "I won't take long since I know you have to get ready. What can you tell me about Chester? How long did he work for Ellen?"

"I think he was with her for at least twenty years. I'm basing that on the plays he mentioned working on with her." Anna looked at Shawn. "Do you think that's about right?"

"Yes, at least twenty years." When Brenda pressed him for details about Chester's temperament, Shawn continued. "He's a nice guy. I don't think I've ever seen him get upset with anyone, not even Ellen. He seemed to take her in stride better than any of us. That's probably how he stayed in that job for so long." Anna nodded in agreement.

"Did you know that he was well acquainted with Randolph?" asked Anna. "He and Randolph knew one another quite well." Brenda expressed surprise at this unknown detail, but realized she had already taken too much of their time, and thanked them for their cooperation. They turned to hurry upstairs, their hands together as they left her. She watched as they exchanged knowing glances and she wondered what else they weren't sharing with her.

Brenda glanced at her watch. Perhaps Chester was avoiding further questions by going straight to Harbor Park from his walk into town. Brenda went back upstairs to the attic and unlocked the door. She pulled a Windsor chair from against the wall and brushed off the dust and cobwebs that covered it. Sitting down, she picked up a stack of papers she had left unsorted after her earlier attempt to find evidence with Phyllis's help. Several folders held scripts for plays. When she opened one, Randolph's lines were there in front of her, and she tried to imagine his resonant voice booming out from the stage. He had shared leading roles with Ellen Teague in most of them. From several playbills, she could see that he had also directed quite a few. She picked up the third folder and noticed a bundle of letters under it. The letter on top was written in a distinct, old-fashioned handwriting and addressed to Randolph Sheffield. The precise script seemed familiar to her but she could not place it.

Brenda examined the letter and found it was still sealed. Could humid conditions have caused its glue to reseal? She inspected it closely and determined there was no way this letter had been read. Carefully opening it, she scanned down for the signature. To her great surprise, she read Chester Boyd's name signed under the phrase 'Your great admirer and good friend.'

It was dated just a few months before her uncle's death. She wondered why it hadn't been opened. Brenda read the letter with growing curiosity.

Dear Randolph,

I can't tell you how excited I am to be coming to Sheffield Bed and Breakfast with the Seaside Theatre Festival next year. I've waited a long time to see what you left the theatre for and now I'll have my chance. Ellen has the cast lined up for "The Rich Game" and I know it will be a hit. Best of all, I will be playing a role in it for the first time. My dreams of acting are finally becoming reality. We aren't getting any younger, Randolph, as we both know, and this has been my lifelong dream. This may well be my last chance. I realize working next to Ellen won't hurt my chances either.

I am happy that Sweetfern Harbor will host the theatre festival. It will be just like old times! I can't thank you enough for telling me to never give up on my dreams. I may not be as talented as you, but I am lucky to count myself as your friend. I must study my lines now and so will close off.

Your great admirer and good friend,
Chester

Brenda looked at the dates again. Remorse hit her that her uncle wasn't there to see his friends perform in his beloved town of Sweetfern Harbor. But oddly enough, Chester was so sure he had a part in the play and yet he had arrived as Ellen's assistant. What had happened in between this letter and their arrival?

There was one person who might be able to answer Brenda's questions and that was William Pendleton. As a lifelong resident and a staunch promoter of the arts, he would no doubt know something about how her Uncle Randolph had helped play a part in bringing the theatre festival to town. She recalled how at ease he was with Ellen the night after the play when they shared champagne together in her suite.

Brenda searched for Phyllis and found her dusting in the sitting room. "Do you know if William plans to attend the final night of the play tonight?"

"He decided he didn't want to go, out of respect for Ellen's death. He is quite upset. He was a great admirer of hers." Brenda asked if he was home. "He's at home until this evening. We have plans to have a nice dinner out since the cast will be leaving."

"I suppose Mac told them they could all leave right away?"

Phyllis glanced down at the duster in her hand. "We all know he is wrong about you, Brenda. Once he lets them all leave he will be sorry he did that. They will go on to the next city for their next play and he will have a hard time getting them all corralled again."

But Brenda simply said, "I can be reached at the Pendleton home if needed." She had no time to lose, and immediately left to drive to William's house, her thoughts racing.

chapter eight

Brenda's car wound its way up the tree-lined driveway to the Pendleton home and she idly wondered how many workers it took to maintain the beautiful gardens and the sprawling manicured lawn. The more modest grounds of the Sheffield Bed and Breakfast were under the care of a father and son team who took care of many other business properties in Brenda's neighborhood. Surely this would require a small army of arborists and landscapers, however.

William answered the door and invited her inside. They sat in leather chairs that flanked a massive stone fireplace in the luxuriously appointed living room. He offered her something to drink and she declined. She questioned him about his visit to Ellen's room the night before her death, and his eyes immediately misted over.

"Ellen's death is a true tragedy." He dabbed at the corner of one eye with a linen pocket square. "But I must admit, it's equally sad that your Uncle Randolph missed out on seeing the Seaside Theatre Festival here. The theatre was his life and he never left it for good, even in his retirement."

Brenda smiled. "I had no idea until recently that he was ever in show business."

"Oh yes, he was an actor for nearly ten years and then directed several very successful plays. I'm surprised your family didn't know that about him."

"Theatre may be the reason why my father never talked about him. My father believed in going to a good job day in and day out and making a steady, decent living. I'm beginning to think he didn't approve of his brother's choice of career, no matter how successful Randolph was." But as she said this, she reflected on the enigma of their relationship, since the letter indicated the two brothers were closer than she had suspected. Randolph spilled his feelings to his brother. That said something.

"That's too bad. Randolph's talent showed in everything he put his finger on." William looked her in the eye. "Now what brings you here to see me?"

"How well do you know Chester Boyd?"

"Ellen's assistant? I know him well enough, though I've never considered him a close friend. He was very good to Ellen and put up with a lot from her. She was very demanding, which explains why he always appeared so prim and proper. His was a privileged life, to be that close to someone as famous in Hollywood and the theatre world as she was."

The air seemed suspended for a few seconds. Brenda knew more was coming.

"There's one thing I've never figured out, though. Chester was originally cast in 'The Rich Game' as I recall. I helped the festival with the local publicity. Chester called to confirm the final cast list to be printed on the playbills and the posters and I was surprised to see his name there as well, and congratulated him. I had already ordered the posters when a few hours later he called back to say he had been mistaken. He wasn't going to be in it after all." He chuckled ruefully at the memory. "I had to hurry up and correct the order. His name was gone and Bonnie Ross was listed instead. He never explained what happened and he seemed embarrassed by the whole thing."

"Do you know what role he was supposed to play?"

"I'm not sure of that since the posters listed the actors and not their parts. The exception was Ellen and Ricky Owens, who played her husband. Their names were printed with their photos and roles."

Brenda absorbed this information and cast her mind about, still not sure what to make of it. "Do you have a take on who may have murdered Ellen?"

William looked taken aback, but looked at her directly with a sympathetic look. "I know you didn't do it. You are much like your uncle when it comes to having a gentle personality. I can't see you strangling Ellen with her belt." He smiled. "In answer to your question, I do know that most, if not all, of the actors disliked her. I liked her dearly as a friend, but she was a hard woman to work under. But I haven't the faintest idea who might hold a grudge so severe as to kill the woman."

Brenda thanked William Pendleton for the information he gave her. She didn't feel she could fully rule William out, but nothing really indicated he had anything to do with it. Back in her car she reflected on the detail of the sudden change in casting, and realized she didn't know much about Bonnie Ross. Every other actor might have disliked Ellen, but no one else's casting had changed. Only Bonnie was a newcomer.

It was already early evening and the summer sky was a brilliant dark blue as the stars began to appear. Brenda decided to drive by Harbor Park. The performance was due to end in half an hour, which would give her time to observe the actors from a distance. Tonight, after this performance, would be her last chance to talk to the actors before they left town, and then her time would be up, and Mac would come to find her.

She stood under the large oak tree at the edge of the park

and watched the stage. She picked up enough of the flow of words between the actors to follow the comical scene. When Chester Boyd spoke his lines, he was truly amazing. His diction was perfect and he knew the part well. The audience loved him and he seemed a natural on stage. It had to have been a practiced role. She was disappointed that she hadn't been early enough to catch any of the major scenes with Bonnie in Ellen's old role. She wondered how well Bonnie knew Ellen. With Ellen's penchant for manipulation, had she cast Bonnie to butter her up for some reason? Or had the casting change been merely to spite Chester?

The cast received a standing ovation at the end. There was no Ellen Teague to push to the front as they exited a side door into the waiting crowd. Instead, all of the actors were mobbed by autograph hounds and photographers. As Brenda watched, broad grins spread across every face as they scribbled their names and best wishes onto the photographs and playbills thrust in their faces. A few reporters even pressed the actors for quotes on Ellen's death as photographers clicked away, but they all declined to comment. All in all, it took a long while before the crowd died down and left. Brenda walked forward and congratulated the actors for a job well done.

"It means a lot that we could be here and stay at the Sheffield and reminisce about your uncle," said Shawn. "He never let us forget how important the arts are, even in small towns."

Anna's eyes held joy but also great sympathy. "We hoped he would pull through his illness and be here to see the Seaside Theatre Festival. It would have been like a reunion."

Brenda realized that this tight-knit group of actors was her uncle's adopted family, just as Sweetfern Harbor had become to him later. She looked at the happy faces surrounding her and felt a crushing sense of loss at the idea that she might lose the Sheffield Bed and Breakfast and her uncle's legacy. She wordlessly watched the cast members as they chatted under the starry skies.

Bonnie's face practically glowed as the others heaped praises on her performance in Ellen's former role. As she chatted with Chester about how privileged she felt despite Ellen's death, Brenda was surprised again by how different Chester's face was now. Instead of his usual stony expression, he relaxed and laughed along with the others, just as he had in his role on the stage, in a way Brenda would never have thought possible for the previously stoic and proper assistant.

Ricky Owens came to Brenda's side and asked to speak privately with her. They stopped near the oak tree where Brenda had stood watching the play while the others continued to chat.

"What is it?"

"Word has spread that you are suspected of murdering Ellen," he said. "I want you to know that none of us believe you had anything to do with it. Everyone argued with Ellen when she got to be too much. I mean everyone – except Chester and maybe Bonnie. That woman was not easy to get along with."

Brenda's smile didn't reach her eyes. Aside from the sad fact that suspicions had spread through the rumor mill, she was also worried that everyone except Mac seemed to be ready to reassure her. Not to mention the fact that she hadn't been able to turn up a shred of evidence pointing to any other suspect. Dread washed over her and she realized how precarious her reputation was. If word spread that she was the prime suspect then everyone would hate her for killing the famous star. The blood drained from her cheeks as she pictured her face splashed across the tabloids and she thanked her lucky stars that no reporters had approached her about the rumors so far.

Ricky noticed the sudden change in her demeanor. "We know you're innocent," said Ricky. He repeated it twice more. "I'm sure the real killer will be found and you will be vindicated."

If the killer is found soon, thought Brenda. The clock was ticking down fast.

"Do you have any idea who did it?" Ricky looked away when she asked the question and she could see again the hint of something unsaid on his face. "Please, Ricky, whatever you say will stay right here between us. I just need a lead to figure out who had a motive. My reputation is at stake – and my freedom."

He paused, as if reluctant to admit that he knew something that could help her. He turned and met the pleading look in her eyes and finally gave in. "I'll tell you one thing, but you didn't hear it from me. It's about Bonnie."

Brenda took a step closer to him and blinked in disbelief. "Bonnie? What could she possibly have to do with Ellen's death?"

"She is Ellen's niece. But she would never boast about it. Ellen has been estranged from her entire family for many years, she claims she cut them off but I'm not sure...it might have been the other way around. Anyway, Bonnie pestered her for auditions for years, ever since she was fifteen or so. Ellen finally cast her, but I think there was something going on under the surface."

Brenda attempted to wrap her head around the fact that Bonnie Ross was Ellen Teague's niece. She thought back to her interviews with Bonnie and racked her mind for any detail that stood out, but nothing came to mind. Ricky continued his story.

"I overheard Ellen on the phone once with her estranged sister, Bonnie's mother. She said this was the last straw, and Bonnie had pushed her luck far enough. I got the impression that Bonnie realized soon after that that she had no hope of future support from Ellen."

Brenda was intrigued. "That does shed a new light on things...but I need to bring hard evidence to the police, not speculation."

"I'm sorry I don't have anything more. But it did bother me that you didn't know the backstory about Bonnie and I'm glad to get it off my chest. Maybe it can help in some way."

"Thanks for telling me this." She congratulated him again and they parted ways.

Brenda sat in her car afterward and thought about Ricky's words. She watched the actors as they walked through the park and headed toward Sheffield Bed and Breakfast. Mac is making a mistake allowing them to leave town, she thought bitterly. She knew that most of them had already packed up and only had a few details to take care of back at the bed and breakfast. In less than three hours they would be on the road again. Time was of the essence for Brenda, so she wasted no time in driving back home.

Chef Morgan was busy preparing a light dinner when Brenda walked in. She helped Phyllis carry trays of drinks into the sitting room where the actors would gather before they departed the bed and breakfast. When Brenda entered the front hall, she found Bonnie talking with Allie. As usual, Bonnie was in a jovial mood, talking animatedly with the young employee. Brenda greeted both of them and then asked Bonnie to join her in the office in back of the reception desk. When they settled down in comfortable chairs, Brenda got right to the point.

"I didn't get to see the whole show this afternoon but I heard you performed your new part well, even with such short notice. Congratulations are in order. I'm curious...I never asked you about how you got cast under Ellen Teague?"

The young actress gave her a winning smile and tucked a

lock of hair behind one ear. "I worked for it. I took acting classes and I begged Ellen more than once to give me a part. I didn't care if it was just a small one. I've always wanted to act. She finally caved in and gave me an audition, and I got the part of the hostess of the country estate. It was my big break as far as I was concerned."

Brenda eyed the vivacious young woman in the chair before her. Nothing seemed false about her, but Brenda got the impression that she was seeing a façade. "Did you know Ellen for long?" Ah, that got a response. Bonnie cast her eyes down at her lap and her long lashes seemed to tremble as if she was about to cry.

"To tell you the truth, Ellen Teague was my aunt, though I was sworn to secrecy about that. I can't believe she's gone." She brushed a tear away from the corner of her eye and looked back up at Brenda. "Ellen had no love for her extended family and that included her own sister, my mother. I know Ellen didn't think I had much talent, but I figured if she gave me any part at all I would have a solid foundation for future work." She shrugged her shoulders prettily. "I feel...sad about Ellen's death, but not grief, if that makes sense. We had been estranged for so long and it seemed she barely tolerated me. I know that sounds cruel, but I just can't muster up grief over it at all." She looked at Brenda apologetically. "I don't mean her manner of death doesn't give me a twinge of regret. No one should have to die like that." She shuddered.

Brenda made a mental note of her choice of words. Right now, she had more important issues to cover with Bonnie.

"Back to your audition...I understand you got it at the last minute? What happened to the person who was first assigned to your role?"

Her expression grew pensive. "You know, I never thought about that. Ellen called me instead of me calling her for a change. I was so excited that I didn't even consider who may have backed out. She told me the role came up and she would give me an audition immediately. Everything was hurried along and I was given the part the next day."

"Did you know that Chester had been promised a role in 'The Rich Game?'"

Her eyes widened and her mouth gaped open. "Really? I had no idea Chester was an actor. Though I have to admit he was great in my former role today. He has seen the play enough times to know everyone's lines." Bonnie chattered on about the performance and seemed oblivious to anything else.

Brenda dismissed the young actress from her office and sat thinking carefully through what she had heard. She realized that Bonnie Ross, for all her emotional mannerisms, was innocent. It was the image of Chester Boyd that nagged at her. Something about the man left puzzle pieces of this murder scattered and unconnected. Brenda knew all too well that time was running out for her and she had to make her next move. Instead, she was tempted to call Mac just to hear his endearing voice. They hadn't spoken since the encounter in the backyard and her heart thumped painfully in her chest to recall that moment.

"He's just waiting for me to fail so he can make an arrest." Brenda realized she was muttering out loud when Allie looked at her in a strange way. Brenda blushed. The young girl gave her a sympathetic look.

"My mother has been throwing out theories about who could have killed Ellen," Allie said. "It seems the crowds stuck around to hear more gossip about the murder, which means business at the bakery has picked up considerably. You know how my mother is. Once she's on a mission, she plans to get to the bottom of things. She's personally handing out samples to each customer just to strike up conversations with them."

Brenda smiled gratefully. "I must go down to Sweet Treats

first thing tomorrow morning and thank her for her help. Has she picked up on anything helpful?"

"She just told me that Chester Boyd has been roaming around on Main Street more than the others. I think she looks at him as someone different from the other actors. He doesn't hang out with them. He is sort of aloof, don't you think so?"

Brenda absorbed this, lost in thought. One more chat with Chester Boyd was in order. She shuddered thinking she could sit in a jail cell the rest of her life while wondering if he had been the murderer. His room connected with Ellen's and so he certainly had access and opportunity. Ellen had yanked his coveted role out from underneath him and that was motive enough. He expressed in his letter to Randolph that this could be his last chance to be an actor. And then she still wondered about Anna and Shawn Quincy who often shared soft and sometimes unspoken secrets with one another. Was it more than the usual exchanges between a husband and wife? Anna had also admitted she argued with Ellen before the play. Frustrated, Brenda realized she had to go with the one scrap of physical proof she had uncovered.

Brenda hurried to the attic and retrieved the letter from Chester to Randolph, and stuffed it in her pocket. On her way to the front door, she passed the sitting room and noticed Anna and Shawn huddled together speaking in low voices. Anna looked up and waved. Brenda greeted them and went on her way. Then she changed her mind and went into the room. Both actors looked up expectantly.

"I don't mean to intrude, but have either of you heard anything more that could lead to who committed the murder?"

They exchanged glances and then shook their heads. "We don't have any idea at all," Shawn said. "I do wish we hadn't fallen asleep so easily that night. We both slept again after hearing you and Ellen arguing. Our room is close enough to have heard something but we didn't."

Brenda didn't want to be reminded yet again of the shouting she had sunk to that night. She thanked them and told them she would be back in time to tell them all goodbye.

She yearned to call Mac and get his input on her next plan. Once again, she recalled their last visit under the rose arbor and fought to hold her tears at bay.

Instead, she called Police Chief Bob Ingram.

chapter nine

Brenda looked through the window at the reporters on the sidewalk outside under the late summer evening stars. She would be thankful when the drama surrounding her was over. The reporters had hung around the bed and breakfast in ever-increasing numbers ever since Ellen Teague had been found dead in her suite.

Phyllis came up behind her. "I wish those reporters would leave. I'd like to see things back to normal around here."

"I'd like that, too," said Brenda. "I think we won't have to put up with all the chaos around here much longer."

"Surely you aren't expecting to go to jail." The housekeeper's eyes widened.

"I don't think that will happen. I hope not."

Phyllis looked beyond Brenda. "I wonder what they're up to." Brenda followed her eyes to see several police cars pulling into the driveway.

She excused herself when the chief stepped out of his patrol car in front of the bed and breakfast. The reporters all knew something big was about to happen and swarmed forward as if meshed into one big glob of humanity. Chief Ingram scanned the yard and spotted Brenda waving to him from the side door. The chief waited for another officer to get out of his car and then gave orders to the officers that followed him. They immediately pushed the reporters back to the edge of the property. From where she stood, Brenda knew Mac was with Bob Ingram, though she couldn't see him yet.

Her attention was diverted to Chester Boyd as he stepped out of the front door to the waiting limousine in the driveway. He was carrying a trunk of costumes, and behind him Shawn and Ricky came carrying several cases of props and makeup. She hurried out to them. Chief Ingram and the detective followed her. She got to the actors first, hoping that Mac wouldn't dare arrest her in front of the gathered crowd of photographers.

"Chester, I want to speak with you one last time."

When they were apart from the others, Brenda asked him about his exciting last-minute role on the stage, asking him if he had always wanted to be an actor. She noticed the two policemen waited a few yards away from them.

"I never wanted to act. I enjoy helping with the props and costumes. As Ellen's assistant, I keep...I kept things in order for everyone else." He entwined his fingers together and stood patiently and politely as they spoke. "Your bed and breakfast provided very comfortable lodgings for all of us. It's such a shame and a tragedy about Ellen's sudden death. I do hope it doesn't mar the reputation of the establishment."

"Never mind that," said Brenda, incensed at his lies. "I know you have always aspired to be an actor, Chester. I know because you were good friends with my uncle."

He shifted his stance slightly. "I don't know where you got your information, but none of it is true. I did know and admire Randolph. That part I don't dispute, but I never had aspirations to be an actor. Besides, Ellen paid me very well to assist her." He pursed his lips and made as if to rejoin the others loading the limousine.

"But it wasn't enough, was it Chester? You were at her beck and call night and day. She didn't appreciate your talents. Then when she finally gave you a part, she ripped it away from you before you could taste success." Brenda reached in her pocket and drew out the letter. She read it word for word to Chester. Anger flared across his face as he listened. She looked up at him again accusingly. "This is the same handwriting found on the threatening note in the rose bouquet next to Ellen's bed after she was killed," said Brenda.

"All right, I did want to be an actor." She noted that he had slipped right past the issue of the card in the bouquet. "I studied every speaking part and knew how a good actor sells their emotions to an audience." The resentment seemed to come off him in waves. "I had talent that superseded some of her actors and Ellen knew that. And then...and then she—"

Brenda held up her hand. "Don't you want the cops to hear you?" He gave her a furious, wordless look. But they both knew it was time for the truth to come out. Inexplicably, relief seemed to spread through him and he sighed. The police chief, accompanied by the detective, approached closer. Brenda ignored both and turned once again to Chester. She had just a few minutes to work a confession out of him or she would be arrested.

"And then what? What did Ellen do?"

The normally sedate man's eyes darted from Brenda to the police standing there and then back to her.

"The letter only tells half the story. She approached me in New York last year during casting. Ellen told me if I wanted to play the role of the host of the country estate in 'The Rich Game' that it was mine. She said it was time for my talents to be recognized. She assured me the role was mine." He paused and his eyes darkened with remembered anger, like bright flames in his pupils. "She promised it to me. I even called William Pendleton to tell him to add my name to the billboard posters. He was doing the promotion for us down here. But I could tell she didn't like the thought of me getting above my station," he said sourly. "The next thing I knew,

Ellen came to me and announced she had given the role to someone else. I don't hold any grudges against Bonnie, but that part was meant to be mine. As usual, Ellen relished the power that she had to give and to snatch away at whim. Ask anyone. You saw for yourself what she was like during that ghastly final rehearsal. Her reasons were never understood by any of us, but she didn't care."

Mac started to step forward. Brenda reached her arm out and stopped him. She did not look at him. This was her game and her life at stake. Detective Mac Rivers wasn't going to have the privilege of sharing her limelight just now.

"Tell me what happened." Brenda had patience. "I can see your predicament. She upstaged everyone and cheated the cast out of their well-deserved acclamations. You merited recognition, too, Chester. You waited on her hand and foot. I'm sure you never had a minute you could call your own. And then she took your part away."

Chester looked at Brenda and it was as if they were speaking alone on the quiet stairway landing once more, and not in front of the police and the distant hubbub of the reporters. At last, things could be said once and for all. He was ready to clear the air. "Ellen Teague was selfish. She was a tyrant." He practically spit the words out. "She was never happy unless everyone's attention focused on her. Randolph Sheffield was the best man and best actor I've ever known and Ellen used him like she did everyone else. I know why your uncle left the theatre. He was sick of Ellen Teague. Randolph was the most talented man I've known but she crushed him under her heel again and again. That's why he left, even though theatre was in his life's blood."

Brenda saw the pain written on Chester's face. "I read a letter Uncle Randolph wrote to my father. In it he said he had had enough of Ellen." She hoped he had more to say, and waited, holding her breath.

"I waited on that woman for twenty years. I can count on

one hand the times she said thank you for anything I did. I got her out of more than one crisis when it came to producing plays. I'm ashamed to say I begged her for a role every year when a new play came out or an actor left a role at the last minute. She knew my ambitions. And she told me I was where she wanted me. That was well put. She had me where she wanted me and I was crazy to think I would be anything different than her servant."

The two officers remained where Brenda told them to stand. Brenda knew the reporters at the edge of the property were getting impatient, but this had to be done right. The press would have to wait.

"The biggest privilege of my life would have been to act on stage under the direction of Randolph Sheffield. Ellen knew of our friendship and couldn't stand it. She made sure I was so busy there was no time to even audition for Randolph, and then later she threw it in my face that he never would have cast me." He heaved an angry sigh at the memory. "And then...when she finally told me I was cast in this play, she took it away without a second thought and gave it to an unknown." His eyes closed momentarily and a muscle twitched in his jaw.

"And you knew then that your dream would never be realized under Ellen Teague," Brenda finished.

"Randolph knew when it was time to go. That was one of the great tragedies for the world of theatre, his retirement from the stage. I never forgave her for that. But when she took the role from me, I finally had enough of her, too." He looked directly at Brenda. "There's one more thing I must tell you. Your uncle did have one short conversation with Ellen about the bed and breakfast. It was when he told her his plans of moving to Sweetfern Harbor. He never once promised her she would one day own it – in fact, she mocked him for his choice to move to such a tiny town. But after he left, she laughed about it and told me she would one day get her hands on the property just to spite Randolph and any family he had."

Now they were getting someplace. She mentally willed the officers to stay where they were. This saga wasn't over yet. Chester focused on Brenda and smiled wearily.

"The performance this afternoon was my triumph over Ellen Teague. It was the happiest moment of my life and I wouldn't change it for anything. I did everyone a service that night." Chester Boyd chuckled as if they were simply having a normal conversation. "It was so easy. There she was, almost passed out from the champagne. Her dressing gown was on the brass hook next to her bed with the belt dangling. It was all so easy. I took my time and she didn't even know what I was doing. I even fingered the belt and then got it ready." Chester did not take his eyes off Brenda's as he said these words and a deadly chill raced through her as she glimpsed the darkness inside him. "One strong pull was all it took and I kept it tight on her until she was dead."

Brenda stepped back in fearful triumph, her heart pounding, and Detective Mac Rivers snapped handcuffs on the actor's wrists and read him his rights. Brenda shakily thanked Chester for the truth and turned to watch as Mac escorted Chester through the group of actors gathered outside on the way to the patrol car.

"Break a leg, guys," he said with ghastly calm. "Never forget you are great actors." He and Bonnie exchanged glances. He smiled at her gently. "You especially, Bonnie, don't give up on your dreams." He ducked his head and was quickly settled in the backseat of the squad car.

Brenda was torn between feeling relief and shock at how everything had turned out. She watched the strange scene on the driveway as cameras flashed in the darkness from the photographers gathered some distance away. Now that the truth had been revealed, it seemed as if the actors felt free to express themselves without reservation. Shawn and Anna both mouthed a silent "Thank you" to Chester through the window. Bonnie allowed tears to stream down her cheeks. Ricky nodded as if silently paying his respects to Chester's terrible act. They were all thanking the man for killing the woman they hated.

Brenda watched Chester Boyd's reaction, too. His mouth curved upward in a small smile as he was driven to the police station to be booked for murder. His dream of becoming an actor on the stage, though short-lived, had been fulfilled. Brenda reflected that perhaps his final speech to her on the driveway had been a performance, too. It was his story, the last story he would get to tell, after all.

chapter ten

Detective Mac Rivers finished speaking to the chief as they stood together in front of the Sheffield Bed and Breakfast. He told the chief he would be back at the police station soon. He glanced at the last of the reporters who turned to leave as the scene was now quiet. Under the summer stars, he walked toward the edge of the lawn to gaze down at the ocean as it lapped gently on the rocks a short distance below. He had his work cut out for him. Following leads in a murder case was minuscule compared to facing Brenda Sheffield. He sat on a bench that faced the view and watched the waves lapping against the rocks. He still clutched the warrant for Brenda's arrest in his right hand. He smoothed it out on his knee and then methodically tore it into tiny bits. The wind carried the scraps of paper over the ocean until most dropped into the water while the rest of the pieces stayed with the wind. He hoped he had not lost Brenda forever over his stupid assumptions. She was right when she told him he didn't know her at all. He had made a mistake, but he knew he loved her.

Brenda and Phyllis went upstairs to the guest rooms. Without words, both women ripped the yellow tape from around the suite Ellen stayed in.

"What about the tape around Chester's room?"

"Rip it off, too, Phyllis."

"Have the police got all the evidence they need from this room?"

Brenda shrugged her shoulders. "They've spent enough time in and around these two rooms. I think they have all they need. Rip it off."

Phyllis did as she was told, relieved the nightmare was over. Brenda helped her strip the beds. Without words, she took the bedding to the dumpster and threw it away. On her way back through the kitchen door, Chef Morgan called to her.

"The detective is looking for you."

Brenda sighed. "He'll just have to find me on his own. I have a bed and breakfast to get back in order."

Morgan watched Brenda stop to wash her hands in the sink. "That man is in love with you, you know. This old house can wait," she said gently. She could see the pain in Brenda's eyes but her boss said nothing as she dried her hands and turned to get back to work.

"I've been looking for you."

Brenda was halfway up the stairs when she heard his voice. Her heart lurched. She turned to see him standing at the bottom of the staircase.

"Did you need something? I presumed you had everything you needed by now."

"Not everything." He shifted from one foot to the other. "I want to talk with you privately."

Brenda debated within herself. She decided he should

wonder a little longer about whether she would let him make amends or not. Her heart still hurt, though she could feel it thawing in his presence. "I'll be free in about an hour or so. We have guests coming in early tomorrow morning and everyone is behind on duties right now."

Mac knew that was all he was going to get for the moment. "I'll be back. Maybe we can go down to the ocean and enjoy the breezes and a cocktail?"

"That sounds good if I can get done with everything in time." Brenda turned from him and ascended the steps. She smiled with a certain satisfaction. Perhaps she was giving him the same uncaring treatment he had given her, but she didn't look back.

"Did I hear Mac's voice?" Phyllis asked her upstairs, hoping he and Brenda patched up their differences. If they didn't, Sweetfern Harbor and Sheffield Bed and Breakfast would have two very unhappy residents.

"He wants to see me when I have time."

Phyllis looked at her in slight exasperation. "You have time right now. I can handle the rest of this. Allie will help me catch up. She already got rid of all the flowers that were up here."

Brenda grinned. "I think it's good if he stews for another hour or so, don't you?"

Phyllis waved her dust cloth at Brenda. "Don't put him on hold too long," she said. "But, yes, it probably won't hurt him." Both women laughed at their joke as they continued to work side by side.

It wasn't much longer when she and Phyllis had finished readying most of the rooms. The housekeeper suggested she leave to find Mac, but emotions battled within Brenda. Finally she shrugged helplessly. "What can I say? I'm in love with the man." Phyllis gave her a thumbs-up and grinned when Brenda pulled her cell phone from her pocket.

"Hello, Brenda." She could hear Mac's breathing was a

little fast when he answered her. It made her feel warm just like always.

"I'll meet you down at our spot on the waterfront in fifteen minutes." She hung up.

He realized he had no idea what she meant, but he felt a twinge of joy at the way her voice changed from the cold tone earlier to lukewarm. He told the police chief he had some business to take care of. "I should be back in a little while."

Bob grinned at him. "It's about time you got your head on straight again, Mac. Take the rest of the night off. Chester Boyd isn't going anywhere. His arraignment is scheduled for tomorrow morning." He bent to the paperwork on his desk and waved the detective away.

Mac let his memory guide him to the café where they had met for dinner just a few short days ago. He caught a glimpse of her gleaming auburn hair swaying slightly in the ocean breeze as she stood under a streetlight. She wore a light-pink cotton skirt that reached her ankles and showed off perfectly manicured toes in espadrille sandals. A gauzy shirt in a darker shade of pink completed her look. Their eyes met and both walked toward each other. He grasped her hand in his and without speaking they strolled toward the edge of the water. Neither seemed ready to talk just yet. Mac led her to a secluded spot. Brenda recognized it as the place they chose when they enjoyed their first real date together. In spite of the stunning view before them, both of them thought about the recent events.

"You know, Mac, fame can do strange things to people. I found that out this weekend. All the actors wanted attention and adulation from fans, Ellen Teague more than anyone. So much so, that it turned her into a narcissistic and selfish person." She paused. "I can understand how she drove Chester to his breaking point."

"Circumstances can do that to some people. This week turned me into someone I didn't recognize either, Brenda."

He looked into her eyes and she read the sincerity written there.

Her warm smile turned into a half-grin, and it drew him toward her. He pulled her down next to him on a rock where they had an expansive view of the crashing ocean waves. The moonlight left glittering diamonds scattered across the waters. Brenda leaned into Mac's strong arms, enjoying the moment. He released her and stood up. She was reluctant to let go of the warmth that flooded through her at his touch.

"Don't get up, Brenda. I want to look at you when I tell you how sorry I am that I judged you so harshly. I should have known you are not capable of any kind of violence, much less murder. I know you would have fought it out in court to make sure you kept ownership of the bed and breakfast. I was so wrong. I am sorry and I hope you find it in your heart to forgive me for being so heartless and stupid." He searched her face.

"I forgive you, Mac. I admit I was very hurt. I understood how frustrating this case was. I wished we could have worked together through the end of it. There were too many possibilities of who could have committed the crime. If I hadn't found Uncle Randolph's letter from Chester, I'm not sure how I would have extracted his confession." She smiled. "You are forgiven. Let's not talk of it again. We both made mistakes with one another and I hope we never go down that road again."

Mac beamed and she smiled back with all the love in her heart. Then he knelt down on one knee in the deep sand, reached into his pocket and brought out a velvet box. He opened it for Brenda to look inside.

"That's not the promise ring," she said in confusion. She gaped at the sparkling jewel inside.

"We are beyond promise rings," he replied. "Will you marry me, Brenda Sheffield?"

She wanted to say something memorable in response, but

was speechless. Instead, she nodded her head vigorously to tell him yes. He laughed and slipped the elegant diamond ring onto her finger.

Mac swept her into his arms and kissed her. Brenda melted into his embrace. She had everything: her bed and breakfast, a town filled with people she considered family, and now Mac Rivers. Words finally came back to her. She leaned back from his lips and looked up at him.

"I'm the happiest woman in Sweetfern Harbor."

He enfolded her in his arms again and found it impossible to let go for a long, long time.

more from wendy

about wendy meadows

Wendy Meadows is a USA Today bestselling author whose stories showcase women sleuths. To date, she has published dozens of books, which include her popular Sweetfern Harbor series, Sweet Peach Bakery series, and Alaska Cozy series, to name a few. She lives in the "Granite State" with her husband, two sons, two mini pigs and a lovable Labradoodle.

Join Wendy's newsletter to stay up-to-date with new releases. As a subscriber, you'll also get BLACKVINE MANOR, the complete series, for FREE!

Join Wendy's Newsletter Here
wendymeadows.com/cozy